Books by Janice Hardy

Foundations of Fiction
Plotting Your Novel: Ideas and Structure
Plotting Your Novel Workbook
Revising Your Novel: First Draft to Finished Draft Series
Book One: Fixing Your Character & Point-of-View Problems
Book Two: Fixing Your Plot & Story Structure Problems
Book Three: Fixing Your Setting & Description Problems

Skill Builders
Understanding Show, Don't Tell (And Really Getting It)
Understanding Conflict (And What It Really Means)

Novels
The Healing Wars Trilogy:
The Shifter
Blue Fire
Darkfall

As J.T. Hardy
Blood Ties

Fixing Your Character & Point-of-View Problems
Copyright © 2018
Janice Hardy

All rights reserved. No part of this publication may be reproduced or distributed in print or electronic form without prior permission of the author.

Published by Janice Hardy
Printed in the United States of America.

This book is also available in e-book format.

ISBN 978-1-948305-91-4

Fixing Your Character & Point-of-View Problems

*Book One of Revising Your Novel:
First Draft to Finished Draft*

Janice Hardy

Fiction University's Foundations of Fiction

Contents

1 Welcome to Book One of Revising Your Novel:
Fixing Your Character and Point-of-View Problems
- What You'll Get From This Book...2
- What You'll Encounter in This Book 3
- How to Get the Most From the Sessions 3

7 Getting Ready to Revise
- First, Fill the Holes 8
- Know When to Revise What..9
- Mentally Prepare Yourself for the Revision........................13
- Stay Organized During the Revision.................................15

19 Types of Revisions
- Different Types of Revisions..19
- Revising on Your Own..21
- Revising From Feedback 22
- Revising Overly Revised Manuscripts (The Frankendraft) 28
- Dealing With Multiple Drafts During a Revision....................31

35 Workshop One: Revision Prep
- Welcome to Workshop One: Revision Prep 35
- Take a Look at the Big Picture 36
- Create an Editorial Map 38
- Revision Option: Make Notes for Later 40

Revision Option: Map Out Any Additional Arcs You Might Want 41
Create a Character Arc Map..42
Revision Option: Map Out Any Additional Character Arcs Needed ..44
Analyze the Draft 45
Create a Revision Plan 47

51 Workshop Two: Character Work

Welcome to Workshop Two: Character Work 51
Analyze the Characters...52
Analyze the Character Arcs 56
Analyze the Backstory..58
Analyze the Theme.. 60
If You Want to Adjust the Roles or Number of Characters............61
If You Think You Have the Wrong Protagonist......................62
If You Think You Have the Wrong Antagonist 65
If You Think You Have Too Many Characters 66
If You Want to Flesh Out the Characters............................70
If You Want to Adjust the Character Descriptions....................79
If You Want to Strengthen the Character Arc 81
If You Want to Balance the Backstory...............................86
Revision Option: Ways to Hide the Backstory.......................87
Revision Option: If You Need More Backstory, Not Less.............88
If You Want to Develop the Theme 89
Revision Option: Adding a Theme................................ 90

93 Workshop Three: Point of View Work

Welcome to Workshop Three: Point of View Work 93
Analyze the Point of View 91
Analyze the Internalization...96
If You Want to Strengthen the Point of View 98
If You Want to Streamline the Internalization......................107
Revision Option: Internalization and Voice 107

109 Workshop Four: Dialogue and Voice Work

Welcome to Workshop Four: Dialogue and Voice Work 109
Analyze the Dialogue..110
Analyze the Voice 112
If You Want to Strengthen the Dialogue 114
If You Want to Vary the Voices 120
Revision Option: Ways to Develop Character Voices................121
Revision Option:
Ways to Develop Voices in Non-Point-of-View Characters 123

125 Workshop Five: Word Count Work

Welcome to Workshop Five: Word Count Work......................125
Analyze the Size of the Novel.......................................126
If You Want to Cut Words From the Manuscript 127
Revision Option: Tricks to Make Cutting Words Easier 130
If You Want to Add Words to the Manuscript 131

135 Workshop Six: A Final Look

Welcome to Workshop Six: A Final Look............................135
Are the Revisions Done? 136
Review it Like a Reader...138

143 It's Over!!

144 Appendix

151 Glossary

153 Thanks!

154 More from Janice Hardy

157 Acknowledgments

159 About the Author

Welcome to Book One of Revising Your Novel: *Fixing Your Character and Point-of-View Problems*

There's something both exhilarating and terrifying about finishing a first draft. The story is finally written down, and you've seen how your characters have grown and developed, but you also see all the plot holes, weak areas, and parts you know for sure don't work.

Most of the time, turning that first draft into the novel in your head takes work. A lot of work.

My goal with this series is to help writers of all skill levels revise a first draft, and help you develop your rough manuscript into a finished draft. This series will provide guidance if you're new to revisions, and work as a stand-in critique partner if you're not yet ready to show the manuscript to another person. It will help you determine which revision techniques and processes work best for you, how to think about the revision process, and how to put those skills into practice.

To help make the process more manageable, I've broken the original *Revising Your Novel: First Draft to Finished Draft* into three smaller books. Book One is *Fixing Your Character and Point-of-View Problems*, focusing on character-specific aspects such as, characters, point of view, dialogue, internalization, and theme. Book Two is *Fixing Your Plot and Story Structure Problems*, taking a closer look at plotting, scene and story structure, and pacing. Book Three is *Fixing Your Setting and Description Problems*, digging into setting, world building, and description. At times, a problem in one area could be due to issues in another area, such as a character motivation issue that's really a plot problem, and I'll refer you to another book in those cases. There is also an omnibus version containing all three books for those who prefer one guide.

Please note that some aspects of revision carry over regardless of what you're revising, so there will be some duplication within the three books in the series—such as preparing to revise and getting ready for revising your manuscript (as well as this welcome letter). The prep work sessions and Workshop One are roughly the same in each book, as are the final workshops that look at word count and the entire manuscript—which might reveal issues in other areas you didn't realize you had.

Just as there is no right way to write, there's no right way to revise. It's a process every writer must work out for themselves, and can even vary from book to book. You never know what extra effort a manuscript will need until you see how that first draft shakes out.

For first-time revisers, this can be overwhelming. There's so much to consider, keep track of, and remember. They often don't know how to start or what to work on first.

For seasoned writers, it can be just as intimidating, especially if revision isn't something they enjoy doing.

For those of us who love revisions and do our best writing after we know how the story unfolds, it's still a lot of work. Fun work, but there's still a long way to go from "the end" to "It's done!"

But I'm here to help with that.

Ready to go? Then roll up your sleeves and let's get to work

What You'll Get From This Book

Fixing Your Character and Point-of-View Problems is a mix of book doctor and personal editor. The goal of the analysis sections is to help you develop your book doctor skills and teach you what you need to objectively review your manuscript. The revision steps and options will guide you to the best way to fix any issues you'll find during your analysis.

You'll review the manuscript from the top down, looking at the larger macro issues of characters, character arcs, point of view, dialogue, internalization, and voice. You'll also focus on the pieces that surround characters, such as revising backstory and infodumps, and enhancing your theme.

There's a *lot* of information in these pages. Take it session by session and work at a pace that's comfortable for you. No one expects you to revise an entire novel over a weekend, so don't worry if it takes you more time. Revising a novel is often hard work, but well worth it in the end.

This information is here to guide you, encourage you, give you goals to strive for, and most of all—help you.

By the end of the workshops, your characters will be solid and well-rounded, your dialogue snappy, your point of view strong, .

Whatever your goal for your novel, this book will help you get there.

What You'll Encounter in This Book

Fixing Your Character and Point-of-View Problems is a series of self-guided workshops designed to lead writers through the revision process. Each workshop covers one step of that process, with smaller sessions that focus on individual topics within that step. At the end of this book, you'll have a cleaner manuscript and a novel that fits your vision.

Workshops: The workshops go step by step through revising a novel. Each workshop offers topics with questions, directions, tips and tricks, plus common problem areas within each topic and suggestions on how to fix them.

Analysis: Each workshop starts with an analysis that examines an aspect of the manuscript and helps you determine where any weak spots might be.

Revision Tasks: These go step by step with tasks to do, or further questions to ask to fix the problems found in the analysis.

Revision Options: Most workshops offer multiple options on how to revise that aspect of the manuscript, focusing on the most common problems in that area.

Revision Red Flags: These prompts draw attention to common problems found in early drafts of a novel.

Problems Found? These prompts suggest where to go to solve problems found during the workshop analysis.

How to Get the Most From the Sessions

I've structured *Fixing Your Character and Point-of-View Problems* in a way I find the most helpful when revising, but feel free to adjust the order of the workshops to best suit your own writing process.

If you know what character issues you want to work on already, feel free to jump ahead to the workshops that fit your needs. Use this book to guide you, but don't feel you must follow every last suggestion and do every single option. This is why I'll frequently say, "probably" "likely," and "often" throughout this book, and suggest things to "try," "consider," and "think about." Just because advice or a technique typically works a certain way, every novel *is* different and what you're trying to achieve with it must be taken into consideration when applying my advice and tips.

Different manuscripts have different issues, so focus on what *your* novel needs. If something suggested here doesn't apply, it's okay to ignore it; just be objective and honest about what the manuscript needs. If you feel you're strong in an area and skip a section, but still can't fix a particular problem, try looking at those sections anyway. You might find the answer you need is there after all, for example, writers with strong character-building skills might insert too much backstory or spend too much inside a character's head.

Revising a novel is just as much about studying the story as it is tweaking the text, and the analysis sessions were designed to help you examine your manuscript objectively. Some questions will be easy to answer, focusing on general reminders and clarification aspects of the novel, while others will be tougher and require hard looks at the manuscript. There will likely be times when answering these questions feels too hard or not necessary, but this is where the real work lies—it's difficult to revise a novel when you don't know where it's weak.

The more effort you put into figuring out what your manuscript needs, the better prepared you'll be to meet those needs.

Getting Ready to Revise

Sometimes, you *think* you're ready to revise, but there's often a period between finishing a first draft and starting the first revision when you're "done" with the manuscript, even though you still have a few tasks left to do. You're tired of drafting; you want to move on to revising and get the novel out the door.

This can be a dangerous time, because if you jump in before the manuscript is truly finished, you'll create more work for yourself. The rougher that first draft is, the more prep work you might need to do. However, if you tend to write clean first drafts, you might indeed be ready to move forward and start your revisions.

Be objective and honest. The more truthful you are regarding the state of your draft, the better prepared you'll be to revise it.

Take a little time and finish a not-quite-done-yet-draft (if needed), run it through your beta readers, get organized, and mentally prepare for all the work you're about to do.

First, Fill the Holes

Look at your manuscript objectively—is it *really* ready or do you still have a few holes to fill? (Be honest.) It's not unusual to have a manuscript with a few holes that you promise you'll "fix in revision." Sometimes you *can* fix these holes while you revise, but other times they need filling before you move forward.

In this session, the goal is to finish the first draft before you begin your revision.

Step One: Finish (or Write) Any Scenes You've Been Putting Off

There are always one or two scenes you know you *need* to write, but never *do* write until you absolutely have to. If you have any scenes you've been putting off, sit your butt in the chair and write them. Even if they're clunky and messy, at least they'll be down on paper where you can fix them. And if they fight you, maybe that's a red flag you don't need them after all (wouldn't *that* be a relief?).

Step Two: Fill in the Details That Still Require Research

Look for places where knowing a detail wasn't necessary during the first draft, but adding it now *will* make the scene richer and more plausible.

Pick a day when you can focus, then start at the first missing detail and take them one at a time until they're done. At the very least, write the information in another file so you can easily add it when you reach that scene during revision.

Step Three: Finalize Any Shaky Character Backstories

Odds are the main characters have decent backstories and histories (if not, you'll deal with that in Workshop Two), but secondary characters—or characters who turned out to be more important than you originally thought—might not be as fleshed out as needed.

Look at your characters and flesh out any missing histories or defining moments necessary to the plot. Now that the first draft is done, it should be clear who matters and who needs more oomph to refine their personalities or personal stories. You'll also know what areas or details will add depth to the existing story and character arcs.

Step Four: Decide on the Final Details or Names

Sometimes you need to live with a name or detail a while before you decide if they're working in the novel or not. And sometimes, you change them mid-novel and forget, so both versions (or spellings) exist.

If you have any names or details you're not sure about, change them now so you can get used to the new ones, and change them again if you still don't like them.

Step Five: Do What You Know Needs Doing

If there's anything you think is going to take additional time or effort, go ahead and do some work on it first. Maybe you know you're not happy about the setting, or you wanted to add more symbolism, or you think the novel needs a subplot—whatever is nagging at you, give in and fix it. Filling the holes now will make the rest of the revision process easier.

Optional: Hand the Manuscript Off to Beta Readers or Critique Partners

Not every writer seeks feedback at the same stage (if at all). If you prefer to receive feedback before you do your revision, send your draft to your critique partners when the draft is done. If you'd rather get the manuscript as finished as possible before looking for feedback, then do your revision first. When (and if) you seek feedback is totally up to you.

Know When to Revise What

Unless you're one of those rare authors who can write and polish a novel in one draft, you'll go through several revision passes between the first and finished drafts. How many passes depends on both the novel and the writer, and you might do as few as two or as many as twenty. No matter how many drafts a novel needs, you *can* make the process more efficient. For example, it doesn't make much sense to polish the text if you're still figuring out the story.

In this session, the goal is to understand the most effective way to do your revision so you're not revising text you've already edited.

Early Draft Revisions

These revisions take the most rewriting, so tackle them first. They change how the plot and story unfold, who the characters are, maybe even the theme, but don't typically affect how the text itself reads (unless you decide to change narrative styles, such as past tense to present tense or first person to third). In early draft revisions you will:

Get the story the way you want it: This is the story you wanted to tell, even if it still needs some work. It illustrates your idea and conveys the concepts you wanted to explore. If the story isn't working, the most beautifully written prose in the world won't save it.

Get the plot the way you want it: Everyone in the story has the right goals and is generally doing what they need to do. Revising your plot is all about moving the pieces around so they're in the best possible places to achieve the strongest impact. For example, you might know you need a scene where the protagonist discovers her best friend betrayed her, but not know exactly where that scene best fits in the novel.

Get the characters the way you want them: Characters change over the course of a novel, and not just in the story. You might start a character with one personality and end up changing it as the novel develops. Or you might decide two minor characters should be combined into one, or kill off a character altogether. Make sure you have the right story people in the right places.

Middle Draft Revisions

Once you've dealt with the macro issues, move on to the text itself. Middle draft revisions include issues that require rewriting on a smaller, scene-by-scene level. These edits don't change the plot or story, but clarify or enhance how the information is conveyed to your readers. In middle draft revisions you will:

Flesh out or cut descriptions: Descriptions almost always need revising. You'll trim heavy areas and bulk up sparse ones, fix talking heads in empty rooms, and generally ground readers in every scene. You'll cut descriptive elements that aren't working to dramatize and/or set the scene.

Adjust the pacing and scene or chapter transitions: A novel's flow determines how readers experience the story. Awkward transitions and episodic chapters can kill the pacing instead of building tension and drawing readers in. You'll tighten the overall novel and cut out any dead weight dragging it down.

Replace weak words and phrases with strong ones: Some word edits require more rewriting than others, and this is a good revision pass to take right before the final polish pass. You'll tweak the text and make sure everything reads well.

Finished Draft Revisions

The final revision pass is all about the last-minute review, fixing the elements that have been nagging at you, or clearing up any messy areas. Most scenes require little more than a cut here and there or moving a sentence for better narrative flow. In finished draft revisions you will:

Tweak little aspects: Minor tweaks, such as moving a comma or changing a word, gets smoothed over.

Drive yourself crazy deciding if it's done or not: We all do it. The manuscript seems finished, but self-doubt nags you and you start second-guessing every decision you made. If it's only general fears, you're ready to go. If they're specific, your writer's instinct is likely trying to tell you there's still a problem to address. Go examine it further and either fix it, or put those doubts to rest.

Read the manuscript one last time: A final read is useful for catching leftover edits or details that no longer apply. It's also good to check the final flow of the story and how it all unfolds. This pass is particularly useful after letting the manuscript sit for a few weeks so you can read it with fresh eyes and see what's actually on the page. You'll make one last pass before you stop messing with the story and turn to the copyedits.

Final Draft Polish

Once the manuscript is working and everything reads smoothly, it's time for the final polish to put the shine on the prose. These edits that don't change the story, plot, or understanding of either, just how the text itself reads. The goal in this final pass is to focus on the copy editing and proofing.

Check for oft-used or repeated words: We all have favorite words or phrases and we tend to use them a lot. You'll read through and trim out anything that sounds repetitious.

Catch any revision smudge: In any revision, you'll find leftover bits that refer or relate to something you edited out. Details change, time of day moves from morning to night, characters refer to something (or someone) that was later deleted. A final read through in one sitting can help make those smudges jump out, especially if you haven't looked at the manuscript in a few weeks.

Check the spelling, punctuation, and grammar: Break out those dictionaries and style rules to catch any technical errors, dropped punctuation, incorrect word usage, and typos—especially those sneaky little homonyms such as their, there, and they're. If you're unsure of a rule or word, look it up.

Check any spellings or details unique to your novel: If you've created names or items, it's not a bad idea to check to ensure every instance is spelled the same way and used consistently. This is a must if you changed the name of anything midway through writing the draft. Odds are you missed one somewhere.

Working from the macro to the micro issues can make the revision process go more smoothly, regardless of how many drafts you do. It also gives you a structure that makes revising a little less intimidating. You know what to worry about when, and you can ignore elements that don't need your attention in that revision pass.

Mentally Prepare Yourself for the Revision

Not every writer dreads a revision, but if the thought of revising is daunting or even frightening, it helps to mentally prepare for the work involved, especially if you know you have a lot of rewriting to do. By the time a novel is written, the characters feel like family, and anything you do to alter that family *can* be rough. Even if you enjoy revising, it's helpful to prepare for it.

In this session, the goal is to put yourself in the right mindset to have productive and effective revision sessions.

Don't Be Afraid of the Delete Key

I learned long ago that trying to force in a favorite line or scene makes that line or scene *sound* forced and it ends up not working anyway. Remember, your words aren't set in stone. You're the writer, you *can* change the text however you want, and that's okay because you're still *writing*. Delete chapters without a thought if they need to go; cut favorite lines if the scene changes and they no longer work. It's still a work in progress until you decide it's done.

It's the Story That Matters

Focusing on the story makes it easier to accept any big changes you might need to do. Plots change all the time, but the heart of the story usually stays the same. Don't be afraid to re-plot or make drastic changes if it will make the story better. The plot is only a series of events that illustrate the story, and you have tons of options for getting to the same place.

⚑ **REVISION RED FLAG:** If you find yourself changing the *story* as well as the plot, you might have a core conflict issue or story premise problem. It only becomes problematic if you're changing the plot and story so much, every revision reads like a whole new book. You're basically trying to write and revise the draft at the same time, which is bound to cause frustration. Nail down the story you want to tell first, *then* go back and create the plot to show that story.

First Drafts Are for Ideas

A first draft doesn't need to be perfect, or even be the book you expected. Stories evolve, plots change, so feel free to move around major plot events to see how they play out. Decide what you want to do, and if you like the new direction, proceed to revise. If it's not what you want, keep drafting until it is. No one says you have to revise the *first* first draft.

Making the Story Better is a Good Idea, Even if it Takes Work

"But that'll be so much work" is a common reason not to make a change, but it's a bad one. You've already put a ton of work into the book, so why not make it the best it can be and give it the best chance to sell? Embrace the work, because "writing" isn't only done during the first draft. Some of the best writing can come *after* several drafts when you can see how all the pieces work together.

⚑ **REVISION RED FLAG:** If you find yourself adding more and more extraneous plot points or story arcs to the novel to "make it better" and very little of it affects the core conflict of the novel, you probably have too much going on. Don't add more to add more—make sure what you add is serving the story you're telling.

Think Macro Until You're Happy With the Story

The big elements determine if a novel will work—the core conflicts, the character goals, the stakes, the premise. If these aren't working, no matter how much you polish the scenes or the writing, the story will feel *bleh*. Major inherent story flaws need to be fixed before the book as a whole can work.

Trust Your Gut

If you think something needs fixing, it probably does. If it nags at you that a certain character does a certain thing, go fix it before you put a ton of work into revising. If that big reveal doesn't have the impact you think it should, change it. If anything bugs you, trust your writer's compass and work it out until you're happy.

Revising taps into a slightly different part of the writer's brain, so the better you mentally prepare, the easier your revisions will be.

Stay Organized During the Revision

How much feedback the manuscript gets before you start revising will determine how much you have to keep track of. Detailed critiques from your ten best beta readers will yield a lot more information than looking at the first draft with no outside comments. How many changes you plan to do also plays a role, as well as the state of the manuscript at the start. Keeping track of it all *can* be challenging.

In this session, the goal is to determine the best way to organize your thoughts and keep track of what you want to do.

Step One: Gather Your Materials

Some writers like index cards and tape flags, others use three-ring binders and highlighters, and still others use software with electronic files instead of manila folders. Whatever your preferred manner, get everything you'll use so you'll have it handy when you need it. Don't forget about the non-writing essentials—your favorite drink or snack, reference guides, links to blog posts with helpful advice (such as Fiction University). If you think you'll need it, put it within reach.

If you don't have a preferred method yet (or don't think your current one is working), try one or more of these options:

Software: Collect all your notes and critiques in one file (or folder) in your favorite program. Microsoft Word's Document Map feature is a handy way to create a table of contents to quickly scan through for what you want. Scrivener allows you to add text sub-files with everything you need right there per scene or chapter. Note-taking software, such as Microsoft's OneNote or Evernote, is another way to keep everything in one place.

Three-ring binders and paper: For those who prefer a more hands-on approach, a binder with paper you can add to and group how you like it can be the perfect fit. You can easily add pages, move pages as needed, and take notes anywhere. You might even have a separate binder for the manuscript itself, with notes and ideas written on the pages.

Tape flags and printed pages: If the idea of everything written and marked on the manuscript appeals to you, print out your manuscript and use different colored tape flags for different aspects of the revision. Tape additional sheets of paper to pages for extra notes, or write on the backs of the pages. Don't forget scissors and tape if you go this route. Highlighters and colored pens are also useful.

Step Two: Gather Your Notes

Hunting through files or pages to find the feedback comment you want to address can be both time consuming and annoying. Collect everything in one place so you can easily access it when you reach that section of the revision. Create a story bible with important details to maintain consistency.

If you don't have a preferred method yet (or don't think your current one is working), try any of these options:

Put the notes into the manuscript file: Copy all the comments you want to address directly into the manuscript, so as you read through each scene, you'll see what needs to be done. Macro comments might be added at the start of each chapter or scene, or in the beginning of the file. If you have multiple critiquers, you might use a different color per person. Or you might use a different color per type of problem to address, such as green for point-of-view issues and red for places where you're telling and not showing.

Create a master revision file: A master file with a summary and list of what you want to revise can provide a nice, step-by-step guide to follow—and a checklist to cross off when each aspect is done.

Print everything out: Hard copies you can physically flip through could be a better option for those who prefer to edit from paper.

Use index cards: A popular organization method is to write out what needs to be done per scene on a index card, referencing page numbers or chapters. You can put everything on one card, or use a different color for each character or option.

EXTRA TIP: *Decide how you'll identify what comments have been dealt with. Delete them? Move them to another file or folder? Change the color, or simply cross them off a list? It'll help when you're not sure if you've made a change or not.*

Step Three: Gather Your Thoughts

There's a reason the previous session in this book is called Mentally Prepare Yourself for the Revision. Revising a novel is a lot of work, and being in the wrong head space can affect how productive it is. It's not uncommon to try to tackle too much too fast, and end up frustrated and feeling as though you're not getting anywhere (or worse—that you're ruining the manuscript). Take the time you need to be in the right frame of mind to revise your novel, review your plan, and have fun with it.

Let my advice, tips, and questions help you focus, stay on track, and guide you through your revision so you don't have to worry about what you're forgetting.

Types of Revisions

Not all revisions are created equal. You'll write clean first drafts that fall out of your head onto the page as if they *want* to be written, and drafts that fight you every step of the way until you whip them into submission and make the novel work. Other drafts you'll write and revise countless times until they become a tangled mess (even though you still *love* that story and *swear* you'll make it work).

Approaching one of the less common types of manuscripts often requires a different tack than the average draft—and a little more effort to make it work. But the results can be worth it if it turns that mess of a manuscript into the book of your heart.

Different Types of Revisions

Most writers will have a first draft that's ready for revision. These will be split between manuscripts no one but you has seen, and manuscripts that have been through a round of beta readers or critique partners. The more uncommon revision will be a novel you've revised countless times to make work and need extra help to finally get it there.

In this session, the goal is to determine the type of revision you're facing, and determine if you need to take a slightly different approach. Feel free to skip the specific in-depth sections if you're not facing that type of revision.

Revising on Your Own

This is a typical first-draft revision, where no one but you has seen the manuscript. You either want to work out all the bugs before you show it to anyone, or you want to make sure it's as complete as possible before asking for feedback. For a more in-depth discussion on this revision type, see page 21.

Revising From Feedback

This is a draft that's been through critiques and has feedback to help guide you in your revision. It might be a first draft or a later draft. The hard part here is figuring out what feedback to heed and what to ignore. For a more in-depth discussion on this revision type, see page 22.

Revising Overly Revised Manuscripts (The Frankendraft)

The more troublesome manuscripts are those you've revised over and over. You've changed so much you often forget what story you were trying to write in the first place. These revisions require a slightly different approach than a typical revision. Until you decide what you want, you won't know the steps to take to get there. For a more in-depth discussion on this revision type, see page 28.

Revising From Multiple Drafts

If you've been revising for a while, you might have several drafts that explore different directions. This is especially true if you weren't sure how the story might unfold and needed to write a draft or two to figure it out. Problem is, you're now faced with several drafts that all contain scenes and ideas you like, and you have no clue how to merge them all into one draft. For a more in-depth discussion on this revision type, see page 31.

Revising Half-Finished Manuscripts

These manuscripts have stalled, often somewhere in the middle of the novel. They require more effort because they're often inherently flawed—which is why they're giving you so much trouble—and until you fix that flaw you can't get the novel to work. You love the story, but you don't want to scrap the whole thing and start over—though sometimes this is the only way to get this type of novel to work.

Preparing yourself for the revision at hand helps ensure you revise your novel in the most effective and productive way possible.

If you've identified the type of revision you face, move on for a more in-depth discussion, or jump ahead to Workshop One: Revision Prep if you're ready to start now.

Revising on Your Own

You've finished a first draft, seen how the story unfolded, and are ready to move on to draft number two and strengthen the story and/or fix any problems you've found. You know what it needs and want to get the manuscript into decent shape before you send it out to beta readers or even agents and editors.

In this session, the goal is to separate yourself from your work so you can look at it objectively.

One of the toughest aspects of writing is the ability to look at your work without an emotional attachment to it. Since you wrote it, you understand elements that might not be clear to readers, and you often overlook any flaws your instincts say need to be fixed. To get the most from a revision, you have to look at your work as if you didn't write it.

Give Yourself the Freedom to Stink

First drafts don't always stink, but a lot of them do, so don't worry if yours is one of them. It's normal. Pretty much every writer writes a bad first draft at some point, and it doesn't mean the manuscript is a failure. That first-draft brain dump can be messy, and the revision is how you clean up the mess.

If you're revising on your own, you have to rely on your eyes and instincts to spot issues and fix them. This can be hard if you're too emotionally invested in the work, and every little "mistake" can feel like the end of the world.

It's not.

As you go through your manuscript, remember: You're not finding mistakes, you're finding places to improve the manuscript.

Approach it as if You're Doing a Critique for a Friend

It can help to look at your manuscript and pretend it was written by a friend. What advice would you give that friend about this story?

Take it a step further and pretend it's a good friend who wants you to tell it like it is and not hold back. They won't take anything you say personally. Then critique the manuscript to the best of your ability.

Be a good friend and be ruthless. The tougher you are, the better the manuscript will be.

Don't Worry About the Time it Takes to Revise

Unless you're on a deadline, worrying about when you'll get a revision done can be stressful and sap your creativity and energy. You want to get your book done as quickly as possible so you can send it out, but rushing the work never results in the best work, and this can hurt you and your novel in the long run.

It's okay if it takes longer than you expect to make your novel shine. And if you're *not* worrying about it, you often wind up getting done more quickly anyway, because all that energy is going into the revision, not the worrying.

Revising on your own is a useful way to get your novel the way you want it before showing it to others. You're happy with it and aren't being influenced during the drafting process by outside advice.

Revising From Feedback

Writing is a solitary endeavor, and it's common to fall in love with your words. You've spent a lot of time and effort on your book, so sometimes the thought of changing a single word can be disheartening. It's even harder when other people ask for major changes you're not sure the manuscript needs. But revisions are a part of publishing, and you'll have to find the best way to apply any editorial advice received.

In this session, the goal is to look at ways to best use any feedback received to revise your novel.

It's important to remember that *you* are always in control of your work. You *can* say no to changes—whether they come from critique groups, beta readers, agents, or editors. You decide how you want to handle feedback, and you might find that you can find ways to satisfy critiquers *and* do something you never expected with the book.

First Look at a Critique

Everyone has their own process for handling critique feedback and diving into revisions, but when faced with pages of information and comments, sometimes it's hard to know where to start. A good first step is to simply read them with no expectations. Make no judgments here. If anything pops up that seems totally out of left field (and there's always something unexpected), let it slide on by.

Once you've read everything, ask your critiquers any questions you might have. Sometimes you'll need clarification on a point, or someone will say something that resonates with you and you'll want them to elaborate. After that, let the critique sit for a few days.

The sitting is an important aspect. You no doubt have hopes and dreams for your story, so any negative comment can trigger a knee-jerk reaction and the need to justify *why* you did something. "They're missing the point," you cry. (For the record, they usually aren't.) Letting the feedback soak in helps you evaluate it objectively.

Dealing With Feedback From Critique

When you get a critique it can be easy (and tempting) to ignore what you don't like and accept only the comments that praise the manuscript. But you asked or the "critique" part, so treat any feedback with the respect it deserves. It was given to help you discern where any problems lie in your manuscript, and to give you opportunities to make the work even better.

Take every comment seriously: Even if it seems out of left field or flat out wrong, someone thought it based on what you wrote. Ask yourself *why* the critiquer said it and try to see the underlying problem, *then* decide if it's a comment that needs to be addressed or not. Often, comments that come out of left field are your critiquers picking up on a subtle problem, but even they're not sure what that problem is. They know something is wrong, but guessing as to the real cause. A totally wrong comment *can* be missing the point, but it's still valid since it's what the critiquer felt. It's your job to determine what made that critiquer feel that way and then decide if it needs fixing.

If you agree with a comment, make the change: Sometimes you'll agree with something, but don't want to do it. It'll be too much work, it'll cause another problem later, etc. Do it anyway.

If you don't agree with a comment, don't make the change: It's your book; do what you think is best. Even great ideas or suggestions can be wrong for your novel. As long as you understand why the comment was made and have solid reasons for not addressing it, you can ignore it. It's the comments you disagree with but can't say why that can come back to bite you.

If you're not sure about a comment, think about what the critiquer is trying to point out and why: Think about why you're resistant to the comment. Sometimes feedback requires an edit that scares you, asks you to change something you love, or even needs a skill you're not sure you have to fix. Or it might suggest something you hadn't thought about before, but there's something in the comment that resonates with you and you hesitate. It's as if your subconscious knows there's a gem in that comment.

If you trust the critiquer had that issue, but know in your heart the scene or detail is right: Sometimes critiquers spot a problem and know something is off, but the trouble spot isn't where they see it—it's all in the setup, so the resolution isn't coming through correctly. Critiquers see the *symptoms* of the problem, but not the true cause, and your gut is telling you they're wrong, but...still right. If you fix the issue where they mention it, you don't fix the problem and might even create a new one. But if you consider why they feel that way, you can trace those symptoms back to where you went off track.

If it's a grammar or punctuation rule and you're not sure if the comment is right, look it up: People remember rules wrong all the time, especially when things such as commas *can* be a personal preference. Overall, if a punctuation change makes the sentence read better, make it. If not, don't.

If it's a clarity issue, fix it, even if you think it's clear: If a reader was confused, something wasn't clear. Sure, you may have left hints, or even talked about it two chapters earlier, but if your critiquer read those chapters a week apart (like a reader might) and forgot a key bit of information, another reader will likely have the same problem. You might not need to go deep into anything, but a quick word or two as a reminder usually fixes the uncertainty.

Do whatever serves the story best: Even good ideas can be the wrong ideas if they don't fit the story you're trying to tell. Adding or doing something that seems cool just *because* it's cool *can* hurt your novel. It can hijack it, add unneeded subplots, and confuse the core conflict.

Don't Try to Do it All

As tough as revising can be, the hard part is reviewing your critiques and not being sure what to do with all that advice. It's not uncommon to want to do everything everyone says, but listening *too* hard can *cause* problems. Sometimes it's better to hear what they're saying and identify the problem that made them say it in the first place.

For example, you might get comments such as:

> *Nothing's happening in this scene, you should cut it.* (This could indicate a problem with an unclear goal, and simply making that goal more clear would fix it.)
>
> *I don't understand why this character is doing this.* Maybe explain what they're really after? (This could indicate a problem with motivation, but explaining the specifics too much will give away the secret and kill the tension.)
>
> *I don't believe he'd do that here.* (This could indicate a failure to lay the right groundwork leading up to that choice, not a problem with the character's actions.)

It's helpful to consider the source when reviewing your feedback. A mystery fan might nudge you to create more mystery or drop more clues, which might not be appropriate for your romantic comedy. The romance fan might encourage you to develop the sexual tension between the leads, even though there's no romance in the novel. A thriller fan might ask you to pick up the pace, even though a historical fiction fan might prefer a slower pace.

It's possible you're getting such comments because:

- The mystery reader doesn't care about characters and only wants a twisty puzzle to solve (and your novel is a character-driven story).
- The romance reader wants to see the two leads fall in love (and your novel is an adventure story with no romance).
- The thriller reader wants an adrenaline rush with high stakes (and your novel is more suspense with personal stakes).

These readers want what the book is not, and their comments would only push you to write a different type of book than what you intended.

However...it's *possible* you're getting such comments because:

- The mystery reader feels the plot is too predictable and she's getting bored.
- The romance reader feels there's no chemistry between your lead characters and they feel flat.
- The thriller reader feels the stakes are too low to make him care about the story.

The details of the comments might be off base, but they point to a problem that *does* exist. It's up to you to determine if the problem lies with the book not being the right type of book for that reader, or an issue you want to address.

Remember, not being the book a particular reader wants to read is not the fault of the manuscript.

On the flip side, you can still benefit from critiques outside your genre. *Would* a little mystery add humor or tension to your romantic comedy?

Maybe tension between the leads in your thriller is exactly what you need, only not the sexual kind. Perhaps a few scenes in your historical could benefit from a little excitement. It's fine to ignore advice that doesn't serve your story, but consider it first.

Trust your instincts to know when a comment is good for your book, bad for your book, or good, but not right for your book. Listen to what your critiquers *felt*, as well as what they said.

But (and this is a biggie)...

If you notice you ignore *a lot of* advice, you might want to examine why.

Are You Ignoring Advice That Can Help You?

Every writer gets at least one rough critique, and it's only natural to ignore words that hurt or sap your confidence. The danger comes when you consistently ignore the very advice that can help you just because it hurts or you don't like it. If you've been revising novel after novel (or the same novel multiple times) and don't think you're getting any better, step back, look at the situation objectively, and ask:

Are you getting the same advice from multiple sources? If a lot of the feedback says the same thing, there's something in the writing or story that needs fixing, especially if it's a larger issue that crops up no matter what piece you're working on. That suggests it's a skill problem, not an individual story problem.

Is the amount or quality of feedback you're getting declining? It's frustrating to spend a lot of time critiquing someone's work, only to have that advice ignored time and time again. People don't want to waste time on writers who brush them off and keep making the same mistakes. If you used to get detailed critiques back, and now you're getting short summarized reviews, you might want to think about *why* no one is bothering to help anymore.

Do you feel as if you ought to do it, but you're blowing it off because "that's what editors are for"? It happens—writers think problems in their work will be fixed once they sell it, and their work only needs to be "good enough" to land an agent or an editor. Not true at all. The manuscript needs to be as perfect and as polished as you can make it *before* it goes to an agent or editor (and that goes double if you plan to self or indie publish).

With any critique, trust your writer's compass. Focus on the story and keep asking what will make it better. You might take a few side trips getting there, but you'll work it out eventually.

Revising Overly Revised Manuscripts (The Frankendraft)

A Frankendraft differs from a draft you know needs heavy revising. It's been cut and stitched together so many times the scenes no longer work together, and the story is either so deeply buried or so watered down that it doesn't make a whole lot of sense anymore.

In this session, the goal is to determine if you have a Frankendraft, and discuss options for what to do with it.

Often, there's not much you can do with a Frankendraft, so be prepared. Your objectivity is gone since so much of the story is in your head that you no longer notice it's not on the page. Sometimes, it's so terribly flawed that it's best to be merciful and pull the plug. But all hope is not lost, and you *can* take steps to bring this monster back to life.

Step One: Say Goodbye

Accept that the Frankendraft is dead and put the manuscript in a drawer. You created this mess by revising it over and over, and it's time to start fresh. Forget the text you already wrote and focus on the *story* you wanted to tell. Rewrite it from scratch in a clean file. No more editing. No more trying to make *this* manuscript work. Treat it as if it were a brand-new idea and run from there.

It's usually worth taking some time at this stage to brainstorm as if the novel you wrote never existed. Take another look at the idea, maybe run through some exercises to inspire the muse and get a different perspective (I suggest my book, *Plotting Your Novel: Ideas and Structure* to help you here).

Step Two: Trim the Fat

Decide what's needed in the story and what's not. What's the single most important goal in the plot? That's your core conflict.

Remember, you're looking for an achievable goal here, not a premise. Something tangible, not a vague concept, such as "the romance between so and so." Look for what the protagonist wants, such as, "Bob wants to win Jane's heart."

What events are *critical* to resolving that goal? If they weren't there, there would be no story. List those events, but no more than ten. Now revise with your core conflict and those plot points and get rid of everything else.

I strongly suggest doing an outline here, even if you're not an outliner by nature. It'll help you see if your plot is working and if you have all the right pieces to write a solid novel without writing the actual novel. If there are glaring holes or problems, they'll show up here.

Step Three: Kill Some Characters

Hard as this will be, eliminating characters will go a long way toward stripping out what's unnecessary. Who is the single most important character in the story (that's your protagonist)? Who is their antagonist? Now get rid of everyone else (don't panic, you'll add some back!).

Make a list of all the other characters. Go through the list and ask if the two critical characters (protagonist and antagonist) absolutely totally need that person to resolve the story goal. It's okay to have a "maybe" list here, as you'll need some minor characters down the road.

⚑ **REVISION RED FLAG:** Watch out for "zombie" characters who might turn this draft back into a Frankendraft—look for anyone who brings a serious subplot with them. If their story risks overshadowing or hijacking the core conflict, they do not need to be there. Save them for their own novel, or cut that subplot out. In most cases, it's better to cut the character as well, so you're not tempted to return to that subplot.

Step Four: Go Five for Five

What are the five critical events that have to happen to resolve the core conflict? Who are the five (or fewer) critical characters necessary to achieve those goals?

Take those five plot events and spread them out over the course of the novel. Which one is the best starting place? One of the critical events in your story should be the inciting event. If it's not, go back to step four and try again. Which one is the ending? You should have figured out this event from step two.

Now, of the remaining three events, which one is the best midpoint reversal event? It should be large enough to sustain your middle, and interesting enough to keep readers guessing. (A midpoint reversal is something that happens in the middle of the novel to surprise readers or change how the story unfolds. It also gives you something to plot toward from the beginning, then deal with in a way that gets you to the ending).

Finally, take each of the two remaining events and put one on either side of the midpoint. These might make good first and second act endings.

You might say, "But I can't do that because the chronology is off now!" but don't worry about that. Just organize and look at those turning points. Is there a way to rework the chronology so that these events fall in that order? Forget what you *already* wrote. Don't try to slip in details you remember you like.

Look at the first event and determine a way to get to the second. Then to the third, and so on. Brainstorm. Think outside the box and imagine what your characters would do. These notes can be rough and sketchy—just try to get an idea of how *this* book can play out.

Those who have trouble plotting might get snagged here, so if you're not sure what to do, try a shift toward the characters and write out their front story. What are their roles in the novel? What do they do? How do they help? Follow their character journeys as if the novel were their story and see what happens. After that, look back and see where this journey overlaps the core conflict and where the plot points might occur.

You'll have a much tighter story and a clearer look at how that story might unfold. You can always add in more scenes or turning points to flesh it out, but be wary of sewing dead pieces back on and creating another Frankendraft. The goal here is to start fresh and breathe new life into the story, not fix the old manuscript.

Most times you have to bury a Frankendraft to keep it away from the villagers, but once in a while, you *can* save it and turn it into something wonderful.

Dealing With Multiple Drafts During a Revision

Some manuscripts go through several drafts before you find the best way to tell your story. Problem is, you can end up with multiple drafts containing good writing in every one. Finding a way to piece together all the best parts and still tell a cohesive story can be a challenge—and risks creating a Frankendraft.

In this session, the goal is to find the most effective way to manage multiple drafts during a revision.

Lists can be incredibly helpful at giving you an overall look at your novel, especially if it's in several pieces. Start figuring out which pieces contribute to your core conflict and which don't. You can hit the critical details in all the scenes you plan to use and see how they flow together. Maybe even use that one-line summary that describes the plot so you can see how they connect to the overall story arcs.

It can also help to create a new file and start pasting in all the scenes you want in the order you want them in. The story won't make a ton of sense since the scenes will likely be disjointed, but they'll be in place and give you a sense of how they flow and work together (and let you see where you might need to write more or cut back). For those using the Three Act Structure, this is quite helpful in determining where your major set pieces fall, and if the right scenes are in the right places. You might find you have too much setup in Act One and not enough scenes for Act Three (or vice versa), and will need to adjust.

Rethink Your Darlings

In multiple drafts, you'll likely have favorite moments you want to include, and you'll probably work hard to get them to fit. But just because it's a great scene doesn't mean it belongs in the final story or plot. Difficult-to-place scenes might not be the right scenes for the book. Forcing a scene can create a stumbling block for readers—it doesn't flow, it doesn't quite make sense, it doesn't advance the story.

This doesn't hold true for every tough bit to fit, and once in a while, you come up with a seriously cool way to make it work that you wouldn't have thought about otherwise. But if you find yourself beating your head against a scene, it might be time to file it away and save it for another story. Look at those favorite scenes and ask:

Does it advance the core conflict? No matter how good the scene is on its own, if it's not advancing the plot, it probably doesn't need to be there.

Does it offer new and relevant information? Often, a favorite scene is similar to one already in the manuscript. The idea appeals to you, and you write it multiple times or multiple ways. It's a good scene, sure, but it does nothing new.

Beware of Revision Smudge

Revision smudge is those bits and pieces left behind that reference something no longer in the story. Maybe you switched which characters were in the scene with your protagonist, or you changed a location of scene, or a goal shifted slightly and the stakes were altered. Reading these scenes feels right, but when you look closely, you realize the details refer to a part of the story that is no longer there. That reference was cut, changed, or moved to a new location. Some things to keep an eye out for:

- Are there any leftover names or details that don't belong?
- Is anything referenced that is no longer there, or has changed?
- Are there extra characters in a scene who aren't anywhere else in the story?
- Is the information revealed new, or has it been added elsewhere?

Check for Repeated Information

Repeated description and backstory often cause trouble when merging multiple drafts. A scene that originally introduced a character in chapter two might now be in chapter five, and readers already know that character by that time.

To help fix out-of-order or repeated details, search for each character's name (or a key detail of backstory) and verify where you revealed it first, then check if it was also mentioned any other place. This can be time consuming, but by the end, you'll know exactly where you wrote what about a character.

Revise Chronologically

Revising chronologically also helps see the story as it unfolds, since you can easily flip back and double check details. Even better, having just read it, the text will be fresh in your mind. You might even make an easy-to-check list of details you changed that need to be edited overall.

Piecing together multiple drafts can be tricky, but a little planning can save you a lot of time and effort, and direct you to the right areas to spend additional time on during your revision.

Workshop One: Revision Prep

The Goal of This Workshop: To organize your thoughts, analyze the manuscript's needs, and determine what revisions you want to do with this manuscript.

What We'll Discuss in This Workshop: How to evaluate a manuscript and determine what it needs, how to create editorial and character arc maps, and how to create a revision plan.

Welcome to Workshop One: Revision Prep

Before diving into a revision, it helps to know what you're working with and what shape your manuscript is in. Novels often change during a first draft, so any outlines or summaries could be outdated by the time you're ready to revise. Your goals for the novel might have changed as well, or even the direction you originally planned to take. Scheduling a day or two to take stock of what you've written and how that compares to your original vision can save you time and effort later.

It's tempting to skip these steps and dive right into the revision, but with all the work that goes into a draft, it's worth the extra effort to understand what you want from your revisions, and the best way you can accomplish your goals.

Take a Look at the Big Picture

You had an idea for this novel when you started it—a vision for what you wanted it to be. Maybe you never wavered from that path and the first draft is exactly what you expected it to be, but often the story changed and evolved as you wrote it. New ideas excited you and your original plan isn't so clear. You need a little reminder as to why you wrote this novel in the first place, and who you wrote it for.

In this session, the goal is to clarify what you want your novel to be.

Step One: What Do You Want This Novel to Be?

This may seem like a simple question, but it's more than "a YA fantasy" or "a futuristic thriller." Do you want it to be funny? Scary? Romantic? Do you want it to fall into a certain genre or subgenre? This is important if you plan to submit it to agents or publishers. Do you want it to entertain or do you want readers to think deeper thoughts? If so, what thoughts?

What type of novel you want to create will help guide you on what aspects to revise, whether it's adding humor, romance, tightening the pacing, raising the tension, or something more fundamental. A character-driven literary novel requires different elements than a hard-core thriller. Just as you wouldn't write them the same, you wouldn't revise them the same. Think of it like adding spice to a meal—you want to bring out the right flavors in your story.

> **REVISION RED FLAG:** If you're not sure of the tone, style, or even genre you're aiming for, or you have multiple (and conflicting) tones and styles, that could indicate you haven't decided what type of novel this is yet. Try exploring the different genres your novel might fall into. Is the core conflict of your novel clear? Does it contain the common elements for any given genre or subgenre? Are the tone and mood consistent with your chosen genre?

Step Two: What Story Are You Telling?

You have a core story about something that intrigues you as a writer, perhaps even a general theme. What core idea is at the heart of your story? What themes are running through it? Forget plot, forget characters, forget details specific to the plot. Think about the general underlying story—at its heart, what is it?

That heart will be the unifying force tying your entire novel together (and often the theme). It will give the overall novel cohesiveness and make it about more than just the plot. Finding your core idea will give you a story compass that will guide you as you revise.

REVISION RED FLAG: If you have no theme or greater concept, don't fret. Not every novel has a theme or poses a greater, universal question. But it *is* an opportunity to make your novel stronger, so it's worth considering how a theme might improve your story. Are there common elements to your story that might further tie the plots or characters together? Is there a greater message beyond the "protagonist solves problem" aspect of the plot?

Step Three: Who is This Novel For?

We like to think our books appeal to "everyone who loves to read," but sadly, that's not true. Readers have their own likes and dislikes, and the better you understand your readers, the better your chances at giving them a book they'll love. Trying to be all things to all readers results in a mishmash of *bleh* that doesn't satisfy anyone.

Your intended audience has varied tastes and needs, and what a middle-grade-adventure lover wants to read is different from what a political-thriller reader wants. If your reader wants a fast pace, you'd want to revise to raise the stakes or tension, cut the fat, maybe add more hooks. If your reader is looking for more word pictures or inner journeys, you might revise to elaborate on your descriptions and character arcs, and build deeper emotions that connect readers more strongly to the characters.

Readers also expect to see elements common to a novel *of* that genre. Knowing those tropes helps you tailor your novel so it satisfies readers looking to read a good tale in their chosen genre.

🚩 **REVISION RED FLAG:** If you can't identify a basic target reader, that could indicate you're not sure where your novel belongs in the market or who it's for. While this isn't always a problem, it can make it hard to revise, because there's no clear direction of what the novel should be. Is it a mystery with romantic elements or a romance with a mystery? Each story appeals to a different type of reader and requires different revision paths. What type of reader is this novel trying to attract? Who do you see reading it?

Once you've clarified the type of novel you want yours to be, you'll have a better idea of what aspects of your manuscript you want to develop and what can be trimmed. You're now ready to examine your manuscript more closely and identify exactly what's in it and how it unfolds.

Create an Editorial Map

Even if you're a fast drafter and completed a manuscript in a few weeks, odds are you don't remember everything that happens in every scene. Without a clear understanding of what's in your novel, it's harder to know the best way to revise. Doing an editorial map (also called an edit map or book map) lets you know exactly how the novel unfolds and where it needs tweaking. It's also a handy reference tool when you need to check when or how something happens and don't want to search the entire manuscript.

In this session, the goal is to map out what happens in your novel to create an easy reference guide for your revision.

As you create your editorial map, keep an eye out for weak spots and scenes you want to work on later. Add revision notes at the end of your scene summaries, such as: "Needs stronger goal," or "Fix character arc." This can make it easier to organize your thoughts for more productive revision sessions.

Please note that this map is to determine what happens when, so don't worry if the plot events don't line up with a particular structure or template. If that's your goal for the revision, you'll fix it during the plot and structure sessions.

How to Create an Editorial Map
Go scene by scene and summarize the important aspects of the novel.

Step One: Identify What Happens in Every Scene or Chapter
Determine what happens in each scene, especially the plot-driving goals and conflicts, as these elements create the novel's plot. You can either list them or just think about them at first (we'll summarize next). If plot mechanics are a common weak area for your first drafts, I recommend listing the goals and motivations of each scene. It'll force you to be specific, and the act of writing them down crystallizes your intent, especially if you have trouble articulating what a scene is about or the goals driving it. Ask:

- What is the point-of-view character trying to do in this scene? (the goal)
- Why is she trying to do it? (the motivation for that goal)
- What's in the way of her doing it? (the conflict and scene obstacle)
- What happens if she doesn't do it? (the stakes)
- What goes wrong (or right)? (how the story moves forward)
- What important plot or story elements are in the scene? (what you need to remember or what affects future scenes.)

🚩 **REVISION RED FLAG:** If you're unable to answer any of these questions, that could indicate you're missing some of the goal-conflict-stakes plot mechanics. Make note of these areas, as you'll want to return to them later when it's time to strengthening these elements.

Step Two: Summarize What Happens in Every Scene or Chapter
Once you identify the core elements of the scene, summarize what happens—the actions and choices made. This will be a huge help in analyzing the novel's narrative drive and pacing.

🚩 **REVISION RED FLAG:** If you can't summarize the action in the scene, that could indicate there's not enough external character activity going on. Perhaps this scene has a lot of backstory, description, or infodumps in it. Be wary if there's a lot of thinking, but no action taken as a result of that thinking. Make notes on ways to add the character's goal back in, or how to possibly combine the scene with one that's weak on internal action.

Step Three: Map Out the Entire Novel

Go scene by scene and summarize the novel. By the end, you'll have a solid map of how the novel unfolds and what the critical plot elements are. You'll easily see where/if a plot thread dead ends or wanders off, or any scenes that lack goals or conflict.

🚩 **REVISION RED FLAG:** If you discover some chapters or scenes have a lot of information, while others have a line or two, that could indicate scenes that need fleshing out, or are heavy with non-story-driving elements that might need pruning. It could even show places where *too* much is going on and readers might need a breather. Mark the areas that need work, adding any ideas that might have occurred to you as you wrote your summaries.

REVISION TIP: *Try highlighting your notes in different colors to denote different elements, such as green for goals, red for tension. That makes it easy to skim over your editorial map and see where and what the weak spots are.*

Revision Option: Make Notes for Later

Get a head start by taking additional notes on elements you'll look at later. Some things worth identifying:

Story questions per scene or chapter: Look for the elements readers will wonder about.

Reveals of secrets or key information: When do characters discover important information? When do readers?

Key moments in any subplots: Add a line or two that shows any subplots and how they unfold. It's also useful to note how they connect to the main plot.

Revision Option: Map Out Any Additional Arcs You Might Want

Aside from the core plot elements, you can also include the pacing of reveals, discovery of clues or secrets, how multiple points of view affect each other, or whatever else you want to track. For example, a mystery might have one paragraph per chapter that covers what the killer is doing, even though that's never shown in the novel.

These additional details can be woven into the scene summary or kept as bullet points or a subparagraph if that's easier. You might even have two or three paragraphs per scene: One for the plot, one for the character arcs, and one for information *you* need, but the characters don't know yet.

This additional information is useful for tracking subplots or inner conflicts, as well as critical clues or what the antagonist is doing off-screen that's affecting the protagonist. Timelines can also appear here if you need to know when events happen to ensure everything works together and you don't have any twenty-seven-hour days. Try adding a simple time reminder at the top of every scene, such as: Day One, Morning.

🚩 **REVISION RED FLAG:** If you discover you have no other arcs, that could indicate there's not enough happening in your novel. A lack of plot could mean you have too many non-story elements bogging down the novel, such as an overload of description, too much world building, heavy infodumps or even an excess of internalization. It could also indicate a repetition of too-similar scenes, creating a plot that feels as though it moves forward, but it's the same basic scene goal and stakes repeated in multiple ways.

The beauty of an editorial map is that once the hard work is done and you have it all mapped out, it's a solid guide to the novel. If you get stuck during revisions you can open it up, see what happens when, clarify where the story needs to go, and get back on track.

Now that your editorial map is done and the novel is clear in your mind, it's time to see how the protagonist's character arc is unfolding.

Create a Character Arc Map

Some novels have strong character arcs (such as a character-driven story about a single person), while others have characters who barely arc at all (such as a plot-driven series). Whichever side your novel falls on, there should be *some* kind of change for the protagonist after going through the experience of the novel. If not, that's a red flag that the plot events don't matter to the life of the protagonist. She's no different at the end of the story versus the beginning.

In this session, the goal is to map out how your characters emotionally change over the course of the novel and create a guide for your character arcs and emotional turning points.

As you create your character arc map, keep an eye out for how your protagonist changes or grows over the course of the novel and where she changes. You don't have to develop a strong character arc if it would hurt your novel, but consider how much a basic arc will benefit the story. You can also develop character arcs for other characters if you wish.

How to Create a Character Arc Map

Step One: Identify the Scenes That Show Who the Protagonist is and/or How That Character Changes

Determine which scenes show important aspects of the protagonist's personality or key moments in her life, especially the events that force a change in views or beliefs. You can either list them or just think about them at first (we'll summarize next).

If character growth is a common weak area for your first drafts, try listing the motivations of each decision that causes change to clarify what's triggering that growth (positive or negative). It'll force you to be specific, and the act of writing it down crystallizes how that character grows, especially if you have trouble articulating why a character suddenly changes her ways. Some things to ask:

- What type of person is the character at the start of the novel?
- What type of person is the character at the end of the novel?

- What happens to create this change?
- When did these revelations or changes in behavior occur in the novel?
- What does the character believe at the start of the novel?
- What is believed by the end of the novel?
- What brings about this change in view?
- What is the character hiding (or what is hidden from her) at the start of the novel?
- What is revealed by the end of the novel?
- What emotional sacrifices are made over the course of the novel?

REVISION RED FLAG: If you're unable to answer many of these questions, that could indicate you're missing some of the motivations or reasons for character change. Make note of any unanswered questions, as you'll want to return to them later when it's time to strengthen these elements.

Step Two: Summarize How the Growth or Change Occurs

Once you've identified the key growth moments of the novel, summarize what happens in those scenes—the choices made and how they affect the protagonist. Aim for showing the direct steps that transform the character from who she is on page one to who she becomes by the last page.

REVISION RED FLAG: If you can't summarize why a character makes a choice that changes her, that could indicate there's not enough motivation or plausible reasons behind the change. Be wary if the change is significant and affects the plot but has no solid groundwork leading up to that change. Make notes on ways to strengthen the motives or add reasons for the character to act in a life-changing way.

Step Three: Map Out the Character Arc

Go scene by scene and summarize the protagonist's character arc in the novel. By the end, you'll have a solid map of where and how the character grows and changes, and what causes those changes. You'll see where/if the character changes for no reason, or where the reasons for the change required feel weak.

🚩 **REVISION RED FLAG:** If you notice most of the changes occur in the last act or around the climax of the novel, that indicates there's not enough growth occurring, and the character is changing because it's *time* to change. Also be wary of any areas where a lot of growth happens in a short amount of time, as this might indicate weak or missing motivations. Mark the scenes that need further development, adding any ideas that might have occurred to you as you did your summaries.

Revision Option: Map Out Any Additional Character Arcs Needed

Depending on how many characters you have, or who is important enough to grow, you might have other arcs to track. Map out the change moments for any additional characters you want to evolve in the novel. For example, you might want to track the love interest arc, or the best friend, or the antagonist. Even if the arcs are small or just show a change in attitude, views, or beliefs, characters who grow bring depth and texture to a story.

These arcs can also come in handy to fill holes or slow moments in the plot, or layer in extra tension where needed.

🚩 **REVISION RED FLAG:** If you discover no other character grows, that could indicate that the supporting characters do nothing but supply information or aid to the protagonist—and often, these characters seem flat because they have no lives of their own.

A character arc map is useful for referencing when, why, and how characters change over the course of the novel. Braiding the character arcs with the plot help ensure that something interesting (and story-moving) is happening in every scene.

Now that you've finished your editorial and character arc maps, analyze what's working in the overall novel and what still needs work.

Analyze the Draft

After doing your editorial and character arc maps, you should have a general idea of where the manuscript is weak and what you'd like to do to make it stronger. Use your maps as guides and conduct a more detailed analysis to pinpoint the areas to focus on.

In this session, the goal is to get a solid overview of where the weak spots lie in your novel, and provide you with the best guide to revise those issues.

If your first draft is clean and the plot is working, you might be ready to revise after doing the editorial and character arc maps (if so, you can skip this session). If the manuscript needs more attention, spend some time analyzing its strengths and weakness and decide what will best serve your story and help turn your manuscript into a nice, healthy novel.

You don't need to fix the problems now—this analysis is for identifying problem areas and directing your revision. Once you know what's weak or missing, you can devote more attention to the workshops aimed at those areas.

Things to look for (potential issues include, but are not limited to):

- **Weak goal-conflict-stakes structures:** This could indicate a plot or narrative drive issue.
- **Lack of character motivation:** This could indicate a character arc or credibility issue.
- **Sparse or missing descriptions:** This could indicate a clarity or world-building issue.
- **Heavy (or missing) backstory:** This could indicate a pacing or character issue.
- **Too many infodumps:** This could indicate a pacing or show-don't-tell issue.
- **Slow or uneven pacing:** This could indicate a narrative drive or pacing issue.

- **Lack of hooks:** This could indicate a tension, narrative drive, or premise issue.
- **Faulty logic:** This could indicate a plausibility or plotting issue.
- **Weak or missing foreshadowing or clues:** This could indicate a tension, tone, or description issue.
- **Areas that need more emotion:** This could indicate an internalization issue.
- **Weak characters and character arcs:** This could indicate a character or internal conflict issue.
- **Weak scene structure:** This could indicate a plot or structure issue.
- **Lack of narrative drive:** This could indicate a pacing or goals issue.
- **Inconsistent point of view:** This could indicate a narrative, character, or show-don't-tell issue.
- **Weak dialogue:** This could indicate an infodump, dialogue, or character issue.

If you're unsure what specifically to look for, try answering these questions (be as objective as possible):

- Is the point-of-view character(s) likable or interesting enough to read about?
- Are their goals clear so there's narrative drive in the story?
- Do the characters seem real?
- Are there strong and interesting stakes?
- Is there too much back story, exposition, or description?
- Is the overall structure holding together?
- Does the opening scene have something to entice readers to keep reading?
- Do the scene and chapter endings entice readers to turn the page?
- Is the pacing strong?
- Are the plots, stakes, and goals believable?
- Does it read well overall?

- ▶ Do the sentences flow seamlessly or do any stick out and read awkwardly?
- ▶ Are the dialogue tags clear?
- ▶ Does the world seem fleshed out?

After the analysis, you should have a good idea of what areas need work. The next step is organizing your notes into a solid revision plan.

Create a Revision Plan

A revision plan helps you get a head start on what you know you want to revise so you're not spending time later deciding what to do. It's a good way to organize your thoughts and look at the overall project before you start, giving you a chance to spot any pitfalls before you stumble into them.

It's easy to get caught up in the story, or worse, chase a new shiny idea that mucks up the novel. The story can, of course, change as you revise, but a revision plan can give you that extra layer of protection against adding more because it's new versus developing what's already written.

In this session, the goal is to help you organize your thoughts and create a plan to revise your novel in the most effective way.

If you made enough notes in the previous steps and feel confident about your revision goals, you can skip this and move on to the next workshop. If you want more organization or guidance on how to approach the revision, continue with step one.

Step One: Condense Any Feedback or Critique Notes

If you sent the manuscript out for critique, read through the feedback you received and make notes of what you'd like to address. Perhaps highlight or copy into a notes file anything that requires broad strokes to fix—such as reworking a scene or changing something on a macro level.

It's also helpful to copy line comments directly into the manuscript so you have everything in one file, especially if you receive several different comments on the same scene. This could point to a slightly different problem somewhere else that your readers are picking up on.

Also review any notes you might have made on elements you want to change. The goal is to get your thoughts and feedback into one place so you can easily review it.

Step Two: Make Notes on Any Revisions You Want in Each Scene

Break out your editorial map and scan though each scene. Look for any notes or comments you made on known problems or aspects you want to work on. Add any feedback from your critique notes, and anything you noted during your manuscript analysis.

Putting these notes in a different color can help immediately identify what to do with each scene. It's also helpful to write out what needs to be revised or added in the scene summary, such as:

> Just as Bob thinks he's zombie breakfast, Sally rushes in with her gun (does it make sense she'd do this?) and shoots the zombie. It has little effect, but does distract it long enough for Bob to get a few inches out of biting range. He yells to go for the head and Sally does, killing the zombie. Bob is happy to be alive, and then panics when he remembers Jane is all alone at the office with these things on the loose (make sure his emotional shift is logical). He has to get to her. Sally takes in the scene and starts yelling at Bob for his poor choice in weaponry and what was he thinking? (Layer in subtext that relates to their failing marriage.) He's just about to lay into her when they hear more moaning from outside. A lot more. (Could this "need to tell her off" be part of his inner arc?)

If this style doesn't appeal to you, take notes in whatever format works for you. If it helps, summarize what needs to be done in each scene, chapter, and/or the entire manuscript.

Even small reminders of problem areas will make it easier to find and fix these areas.

Step Three: Plan Your Approach

Once you know what you want to do, decide how you want to approach your revision. Are you a one-chapter-at-a-time writer who likes to get that chapter perfect before moving forward? Or maybe you prefer one item at a time, such as checking for goals in the entire novel, then looking at description, then looking for trouble words? Maybe you're more of a large chunk of several chapters at a time reviser and like to get one act done before moving to the next. However you prefer to revise, knowing what you'll work on each session keeps you focused.

Step Four: Make Your Revisions

Some edits are easy to do—fixing the typos, changing a name or term, clarifying an ambiguous pronoun. If you need a little warm up before you get to the tough edits, do these first—they take the least amount of brain power and offer a sense of accomplishment. Momentum helps a lot in a revision.

Some revision passes work better when you look at the entire manuscript vs. smaller chunks, so feel free to vary how you review your manuscript. For example, continuity checks are harder to do in chunks, since you might forget what happened between reads. Reading the manuscript in a short timeframe keeps the details fresh in your mind and makes it easier to spot where something is off.

After you're done, re-read your notes and critiques to see if you've addressed everything you wanted to. Double check any feedback that you ignored to see if you have a new opinion on it now (it happens). Tweak as needed.

Step Five: Gain Some Perspective

Once the revision is done, schedule some downtime so the manuscript can sit for a while and the details can fade from your memory. I like to give it a month, but aim for at least a week, longer if the changes were extensive. You want to give your brain time to forget what *was* there so when you look at it again, you'll see what *is* there. There's always some revision smudge that slips into the text that refers to something that changed or was cut.

When you're ready, read through the manuscript once more and make any changes that jump out. Most of it will likely be small edits, a word change here and there. It's not uncommon to cut sentences or even paragraphs that slow the story down now that you've been away and can spot the dead weight. However, if you're still making large changes and rewriting sections, you might consider going back to step four and reworking those trouble spots.

Step Five: Polish the Manuscript

After the story is as good as you can make it, it's time to polish the text until it shines. This is where you'll address individual word choices, copyedits, and grammar goofs you might have made. These elements don't affect the story, but focus on the technical aspects of writing.

Don't be afraid to mix it up or change the order of these steps if that works for you. Some folks might prefer to do the larger issues first and finish up with the easy edits and that's okay. The whole goal of a revision plan is to keep you focused and provide a way to track your progress.

Now that you've refreshed the intricacies of your story in your mind, and planned out what needs tweaking and how you want to approach it, it's time to move on to the manuscript itself.

Let's look at our characters and see what they need to become better story people.

Workshop Two: Character Work

The Goal of This Workshop: To ensure you have strong, memorable characters readers will love, or love to hate if that's the goal.

What We'll Discuss in This Workshop: How to analyze the characters and character arcs for weaknesses, and discover ways to strengthen those weaknesses. We'll take a look at overall character development, character arcs, backstory, character description, and theme.

Welcome to Workshop Two: Character Work

There's an old saying: plot might bring readers to our stories, but characters keep them there. This underscores the importance of well-crafted, compelling characters in a novel. One of the most common reasons readers put a book down is, "I didn't like the main character." This is why I like to tackle them first during a revision. Amazing characters can overcome other writing flaws, so it takes some of the pressure off (just a little though—you don't want to slack off on the rest of the novel).

How much revising you'll need to do with your characters depends on how much work went into them beforehand. Character-focused writers will likely be strong in this area, requiring little tweaking to bring their characters to life, or they might have gone overboard and need to reel some of that information back in. Plot-focused writers typically find character development a weak area, and need to spend extra time fleshing out the characters now that they know how the novel unfolds.

No matter which side you fall on, the goal of this workshop is to strengthen weak characters and fix character issues found during your manuscript analysis.

Analyze the Characters

You often see two kinds of characters in a first draft: shallow ones who did what they were told without caring why, and overly developed ones who are too wrapped up in their own lives to pay attention to what you wanted them to do. One side needs development, the other needs some personality pruning.

In this session, the goal is to analyze your characters and determine which ones need further development and which ones need pruning.

In the next sessions, you'll also look at the character arcs, backstory, and theme.

If you think your characters aren't living up to their full potential, analyze who they are and how they fit into the story. Look for any characters who aren't pulling their weight, might not be needed, or who need more development to turn them into three-dimensional people.

At this stage, focus on analyzing what you want to do and making notes to guide you afterward.

Run through some basic character questions and determine where the weak spots lie. Start with the most important character (the protagonist) and work your way to the smaller ones, so you'll have a better understanding of what traits will support and/or conflict with your main characters.

If you already know what's missing from the characters, then jump right into your revision session.

Step One: Determine if the Right Characters Are in Place

Though it's rare, sometimes you write an entire novel and realize you had the wrong characters. The protagonist is wrong, the antagonist is flimsy, or a smaller, throwaway character turns out to be the most important person in the story. Sometimes you *have* the right character, but the personality is throwing off the whole novel.

Go through the following questions to see if the novel has the right characters for the story you want to tell:

▶ **Do you have the right protagonist for this story?** The right protagonist has a strong reason to drive the plot, and the story would fall apart or change significantly if this person wasn't part of the tale.

▶ **Do you have the right antagonist for this story?** The right antagonist has good reasons for acting, and is in conflict with the protagonist. She's also a worthy foe for the protagonist to ensure every win is earned.

▶ **Do you have the right number of characters?** Readers can keep track of only so many people at a time. Too many characters make it hard for readers to follow the story; too few make it feel coincidental or contrived.

The right characters in the right places can make the story world feel real and plausible, and create compelling people a reader wants to follow.

🚩 **REVISION RED FLAG:** Pay attention to any characters who showed up as weak on your character arc map, or who don't seem to do a lot for the story. Also note any characters you don't immediately remember who they are and what they do. Those are strong candidates for cutting.

Problems Found?

If you find the wrong characters or number of characters, spend some time doing the exercises in If You Want to Adjust the Roles or Number of Characters on page 61.

Step Two: Determine if the Characters Are Working Overall

Readers don't typically enjoy reading about people they don't like (though people do seem to enjoy *watching* characters they don't like. Go figure). An unlikable character is a major reason novels don't work, so pinpoint what it is about your characters (especially your main characters) that will connect with readers. Make sure they're people readers can relate to, sympathize with, or be fascinated by.

Go through the following questions and see if the characters are the kind of people readers will want to read about:

- **Do you like the point-of-view character(s) or find them interesting?** If the main characters aren't piquing interest or tugging heartstrings, they'll need a little more development. Pay particular attention to the protagonist and antagonist. Is their story worth reading about? Are *they* worth reading about?

- **Do you care about these characters enough to read their story?** This can be tough for the author to answer, since we usually love our creations, but look at it objectively. Did you give readers a reason to care about the people in your story? Are they worth rooting for? If you didn't know their backstory, would you still care? Remember, readers don't know what you know about these people.

- **Do the characters seem real?** Readers will suspend disbelief for a novel they want to read, but when characters feel flat, fake, or downright ridiculous, it yanks them out of the story. Characters who act in ways a normal person never would strain reader credibility, as do too-perfect characters who never make mistakes and always have situations work out for them. "Real" can be subjective depending on the genre, but make sure your characters are being true to the people you've created.

- **Are the characters believable in their roles?** You don't want to have an expert hacker who gets technical terms wrong, or a world-renowned neurosurgeon who's only seventeen. Readers aren't going to buy a character who flies in the face of plausibility. If there's anything about your characters that stretches credibility, or relies on specific knowledge they wouldn't have, take the time to ensure they're believable in that role.

- **Are the characters flawed in ways that affect their decisions in the story?** Flaws make characters feel real and help readers connect to them. They're also key elements in developing the plot, as flaws often cause a character to make mistakes, and determine what a character needs to overcome to win in the climax.
- **Do they have virtues that affect their decisions in the story?** Characters need both good and bad traits. Virtues guide them, even if they're doing the wrong thing for the right reasons. No matter how bad a character might be, there's something redeemable deep inside.
- **Do they have contradicting beliefs, both with themselves, and the other characters?** Inconsistency is part of life, and characters can (and should) have conflicting beliefs and opinions. If everyone believes the same thing, there's little room to develop the conflict necessary for the plot. Be wary though, if the contradictions stretch credibility.

⚑ **REVISION RED FLAG:** Pay attention to any characters you could get rid of and not miss, as well as any who feel as though they're acting out the plot because you told them to. Aim for three-dimensional characters with strengths and weakness, interesting stories, and intriguing conflicts.

Problems Found?

If you find any flat or boring characters, spend some time doing the exercises in If You Want to Flesh Out the Characters on page 70.

Step Three: Determine if the Character Descriptions Are Working

Part of bringing characters to life is describing them to your readers, but it's not uncommon to get the balance off in a first draft.

Go through the following questions and see if your characters could use a little more, or less, description.

- **How much physical description do you want?** How much you describe your characters is a matter of personal taste. You might be satisfied with one or two brief physical details, or you might paint a word portrait for each character.

- **Are the main characters adequately described?** Readers should be able to get a good sense of who these people are, and typically, what they look like.
- **Is there too much focus on physical details?** If every character has a long list of physical traits and not a lot on who they are as a person, that could indicate weak character development.
- **Are the secondary characters described?** If all the focus is on the major characters, secondary characters might be poorly drawn or underdeveloped. While you don't want to go overboard, you want them to feel solid in readers' minds.
- **How many details do you use to describe the various characters?** Look at the level of detail in your character hierarchy. Major characters typically have the most description, then it lessens as the importance of the character lessens. If your walk-on characters have the same level of description as your protagonist, that could indicate description that slows the pace or derails the narrative drive.
- **Do the descriptions all fit the same format?** Sometimes you get into a pattern with descriptions, describing every character in the same fashion, such as one or two sentences listing off height, age, hair and eye color each time a new character is introduced.

⚑ **REVISION RED FLAG:** Beware of generic physical details that read like something you'd fill out at the DMV.

Problems Found?

If you find the descriptions need work, spend some time doing the exercises in If You Want to Adjust the Character Descriptions on page 79.

Analyze the Character Arcs

The type of novel you have determines how strong the character arc is. Stories focusing on deeply personal character struggles (such as romance or literary fiction) typically have a much stronger character arc driving the plot, while stories that focus on the plot (such as thrillers or mysteries) usually have less need for the characters to grow and change. The strength of a solid character arc is that it overlays beautifully with the plot, providing the necessary tension and motivation for events to unfold. It fills any slow spots in the external plot, and allows you more flexibility in how you handle your pacing.

In this session, the goal is to analyze your protagonist's character arc to ensure it's working the way you want it to. Do this for as many additional characters as you'd like.

In the next sessions, you'll look at your backstory and theme.

Determine if the Character Arcs Are Working

Just as there are major turning points in a plot, there are major turning points in a character arc. These often coincide with major plot moments, and might even be the source of the action, the problem facing the characters, or the conflict tearing them apart.

If you mapped out the character arcs for the novel, you should have a good idea of where the emotional turning points fall and what areas could use more work (if you haven't, I recommend going back to Workshop One and doing the Create a Character Arc Map session).

Go through the following questions to determine if your protagonist has a character arc, and if that arc is achieving the emotional growth you want for the novel.

- ▶ **What does the protagonist learn over the course of the novel?** The character ought to change in some way between the opening and the ending (some exceptions apply, such as a genre series).
- ▶ **How does the internal conflict affect that growth?** Overcoming the internal flaw or weakness causes the character to grow.
- ▶ **What lie is she telling herself or does she believe at the start of the novel?** Frequently, the character believes a lie about something affecting her life and happiness.
- ▶ **When does she realize it is or isn't true?** The realization of the truth is often a pivotal moment in the character arc, leading to the needed growth that allows the protagonist to win in the climax.
- ▶ **What does she want most of all as a person?** For the character arc, this is usually something emotional and internal, not the external goal that drives the plot.

- **Does the external plot facilitate her achieving this personal desire?** It's by going through the external plot that the internal change occurs.
- **What is she most afraid of?** This will help develop or clarify the conflicts she'll likely face in the story.
- **When does she face this fear?** This traditionally happens shortly before the climax, or during the climax itself. It's often the trigger for fully realizing that growth.
- **Where do the turning points of the growth occur?** These should be spread out over the course of the novel.

Depending on how character-focused the novel is, you might also ask these questions of the other characters. The antagonist, secondary, and supporting characters can have arcs as well, and conflicting arcs add tension to a novel. Look for any scenes in your revision plan that need more tension and consider if an arc turning point would help them. Arcs get other characters more involved in the plot and add depth and richness to the story.

REVISION RED FLAG: If you notice most of these moments exist at the end of the novel, that could indicate that the characters aren't growing, but just change because the book is over. The growth will likely feel false to readers since the characters haven't earned that growth. Try spreading the moments (and growth) out over the course of the novel so the lessons learned are natural to the plot. Use your outline and major turning points to make sure you have gradual and consistent growth.

Problems Found?

If you find any too-static or changes-too-quickly characters, spend some time doing the exercises in If You Want to Strengthen the Character Arc on page 81.

Analyze the Backstory

When done well, backstory can add depth and meaning to a novel. When done poorly, it can bog down the plot, muck up the story, and ruin the pacing, which is why finding the right balance in your novel is critical.

In this session, the goal is to determine how your backstory affects your novel and if you need to cut, add, or revise any of it.

In the next session, you'll look at your theme.

Determine if the Backstory is Working

Despite the common advice that says eliminate all backstory, backstory is not a bad thing on its own. It's only when it hurts the novel that it becomes a problem.

Look at the backstory in your scenes (especially in the first 25 percent of the novel) and decide what information is vital to understand each scene and what isn't.

- **Is the backstory relevant to the scene?** Backstory works when there's a reason to have it. If knowing this information does nothing to advance the scene, it can usually go.
- **Does this information help readers understand what's going on in this scene?** If readers will be lost if they don't know this information, it can likely stay.
- **Will knowing this information hurt the tension or mystery of the scene (or story)?** If learning the history or details of the backstory too early will *answer* questions you hoped would hook readers and keep them reading, it's usually better to cut those early details and let the mystery build.
- **What would be lost in this scene if you took the backstory out?** If losing the backstory has no affect on the scene, go ahead and toss it.
- **Why do *you* want it in the scene?** Sometimes your subconscious is trying to tell you to add something to a scene. If a bit of backstory *needs* to be there, take a few minutes to understand why. Often, the backstory is key to how the character feels in the current scene and what she'd do or say. You might be able to add that missing element without the backstory—or discover the backstory does indeed need to stay.

   REVISION RED FLAG: One of the problems with backstory is that you often think readers "need to know" this information to "really get" the character, so you dump in way more than readers want, let alone need. Yet, wondering *about* a character's history is often what keeps readers reading and pulls them deeper into the novel. For example, if the protagonist has had troubles with the police, then you might show her avoiding an officer on the street, or taking special care to not let an officer see her face. Readers will wonder, "Why is she avoiding the cops?" and be intrigued to read on. If you say right away that the protagonist has a warrant out for her arrest (or worse, what it's for), then there's no mystery anymore.

Problems Found?

If you find heavy or missing backstories, spend some time doing the exercises in If You Want to Balance the Backstory on page 86.

Analyze the Theme

Theme and characters go hand in hand, because people often seek greater meaning in (or through) their actions. We want what we do to matter, and what a character does creates an entire plot. A plot that matters typically has a strong theme running through it that connects it to the character arc.

In this session, the goal is to examine your theme and see how it's working with your characters and plot.

Determine if the Theme is Working

Not every novel has a theme, but even in an action-focused plot, there's usually *something* bigger underneath—it's not just a series of scenes strung together to solve a problem. The connection could be as basic as "revenge" or "justice," or as complicated as, "Are we truly human if we perform inhumane acts?" Identifying the underlying concept behind the story helps you understand what the book is "about" on a grander scale.

Take a minute and consider:

- **What is the theme (or themes) of this story?** Look for common ideas or concepts repeated throughout the novel.
- **Where examples of this theme are found in the novel?** This helps identify important plot or character arc moments, and even helps

judge if the novel is too heavy on the internal journey and light on plot (or vice versa).

▶ **Where and how does the theme deepen the character arcs?** The theme is often illustrated by the character arc.

▶ **How does the theme tie into the resolution of the novel?** It's not uncommon for the climax to show everything the protagonist has learned and how she's grown, reflecting the theme and tying the external and internal conflicts together.

🚩 **REVISION RED FLAG:** Be wary of too many themes fighting for attention in your novel. If the story is about *everything*, then it's not likely to delve deep enough into any one idea to resonate with readers.

Problems Found?

If you find any theme issues (or you're missing a theme), spend some time doing the exercises in If You Want to Develop the Theme on page 89.

If You Want to Adjust the Roles or Number of Characters

Finding the right balance among characters can be tricky, but once you know how the story unfolds, it's easier to see who is doing their job and who needs to be let go. Characters you originally felt were critical turn out not to be, and those you used because you needed a body in a scene end up becoming major characters. And then there are the harder-to-fix issues—having the totally wrong character in a critical role.

The right number of characters in a novel is also subjective. An epic fantasy series is going to have more characters than a contemporary stand-alone piece. Even making a list of your characters isn't always helpful, because many will be walk-on or throwaway characters, and knowing that, they carry less weight in a list. You might not even list them because they're so unimportant, yet they take up valuable room in the reader's memory.

The following sessions will help determine if you have issues with the wrong protagonist, antagonist, or too many characters. Naturally, if you don't think you have a problem in one of these areas, skip that session.

If You Think You Have the Wrong Protagonist

The wrong protagonist is a serious issue for a first draft, but one that does happen from time to time. You have an idea, you write it, and it turns out that the person you thought was at the center of everything really isn't.

In this session, the goal is to find the right protagonist for your story, or a way to rework your protagonist to fit the story.

Step One: Determine Who Has the Problem

Look at the core conflict of your novel and identify any characters severely affected by that problem. If the goal of the novel is to resolve this problem, the protagonist will be the one trying to do so. List all the characters affected.

To fix the existing protagonist: Look for ways to make the core conflict problem apply to the protagonist. How is this problem going to make her life worse?

Step Two: Determine Who Has the Ability to Act

Some problems affect everyone even if they can't do anything about them. Cross off any characters who can't affect the problem. Look next at characters who *are* in a position to do something about it. Maybe they have access, or skills, or know the right people to help solve the problems.

To fix the existing protagonist: Look for ways to make the protagonist able to affect a change.

Step Three: Determine Who Has Reasons to Act

Being able to act is only the first step. A good protagonist also has *reasons* to act to resolve that core conflict. Cross off anyone who doesn't have a personal reason to solve the problem.

To fix the existing protagonist: Look for ways to add a personal motivation to the protagonist.

Step Four: Determine Who Has Something to Lose

If there's nothing to lose, there's nothing to gain, and a lack of stakes is a common problem with weak protagonists. First, make sure failing to resolve the problem *has* consequences, then, cross off anyone who won't lose something important if they fail.

To fix the existing protagonist: Look for ways to give the protagonist personal stakes and serious consequences if she fails to resolve the problem.

Step Five: Determine Who Has Something to Gain

Winning isn't winning if there's no reward (at least in stories). A good protagonist gains something valuable by resolving the novel's problem. Often, it's connected to the character arc and will allow her to be happy. Get rid of any potential protagonists who don't have anything to gain by winning.

To fix the existing protagonist: Look for ways the protagonist will benefit from solving the problem, especially if it also fits into her character arc (if the protagonist has no character arc, that could be why the character isn't working).

Step Six: Determine Who Has Capacity to Change

In most stories, the protagonist goes through the experiences in the novel and is changed for the better (the character arc). Cut any characters from the list who are the same people at the end of the story as they are at the beginning.

To fix the existing protagonist: Look for ways to cause a change in the protagonist. The problems overcome should have a long-lasting effect (you might need to do the character arc exercises for this character).

Step Seven: Determine Who Has a Compelling Quality

Protagonists have something about them that makes readers want to read about them. It could be a skill, a power, an attitude, or even a way of thinking. Cross off any character without that "something special" about them.

To fix the existing protagonist: Look for ways to make the protagonist more compelling. Add a trait or characteristic to make her more interesting.

Step Eight: Determine Who Has an Interesting Flaw

Flaws provide areas for growth, so perfect characters can leave the room. A good protagonist needs a flaw to make her human, and give her something to work on to better herself.

To fix the existing protagonist: Look for ways to give the protagonist flaws that connect to her character arc and the problem at hand.

Step Nine: Determine Who Has Someone or Something Interesting in the Way

The protagonist is only as good as the antagonist in her way. Look at the remaining potential protagonists and get rid of everyone who doesn't have someone or something trying to stop them.

To fix the existing protagonist: Look for ways to give the protagonist a worthy foe to overcome.

Step Ten: Choose Your Protagonist

Look at the list of remaining characters. Hopefully it's a small list (if not, go through these questions again and be more specific and personal about the answers as they pertain to your core conflict). Pick the best candidate to drive your story and put him or her back in as the protagonist. Rework the overall story as needed before returning to the rest of the revision.

To fix the existing protagonist: Is your protagonist now the right person for the story? If so, revise overall to fix the problem areas revealed in the questions. If not, and you're *sure* this is indeed the right person, then the issue might not be the protagonist but the core conflict or premise of the novel.

If You Think You Have the Wrong Antagonist

Having the wrong antagonist is a little more common in a first draft, because you often know the general "badness" of your story problem, but not exactly who will fill that role. You might even wind up with a cardboard villain who's evil for the sake of being evil—which usually results in a boring story without any real conflict or stakes.

In this session, the goal is to find the right antagonist for your story, or fix the existing antagonist to be a better foil for your hero.

Step One: Determine Who Caused the Problem

Look at your core conflict and list any characters (whether they're in the story or not) who created this problem, either directly or indirectly.

To fix your existing antagonist: Look for ways to make the antagonist responsible for the problem.

Note: The antagonist doesn't cause *every* story core conflict, but they will at least try to take advantage of it.

Step Two: Determine Who Benefits From the Problem

Antagonists act with the end game in mind. Cross off anyone who doesn't benefit from this problem.

To fix your existing antagonist: Look for ways to make the antagonist benefit from the problem.

Step Three: Determine Who is Motivated to Cause This Problem

Nobody is bad just to be bad—they have reasons, even if those reasons are twisted and hardly make sense to anyone but them. Cut any characters who have no reason to want to see this problem happen or hurt the protagonist.

To fix your existing antagonist: Look for ways to motivate the antagonist to want to see the problem occur.

Step Four: Determine Who Has Reason to Prevent the Protagonist From Acting

In most cases, the antagonist has a personal reason to keep the protagonist from resolving the problem and fixing whatever is wrong. Get rid of any potential antagonists who don't have *some* reason to stop the protagonist.

To fix your existing antagonist: Look for ways to put the antagonist in direct conflict with the protagonist. Make sure their goals are at odds with one another.

Step Five: Identify Your Antagonist

The antagonist should be the only one left on the list, but if you have several options, pick the one who's the most compelling overall. If the list is still long, go through the questions again with more personal and specific answers that pertain to the conflict.

To fix your existing antagonist: Is your antagonist now the right person for the story? If so, revise overall to fix the problem areas revealed in the questions. If not, and you're *sure* this is the right antagonist, the problem might not be the antagonist, but the core conflict or premise of the novel.

If You Think You Have Too Many Characters

The number of characters in a novel tends to grow as you write it. You discover scenes need extra hands, or a walk-on role turns out to be a fantastic secondary character, or, if you're writing a series, after a few books you realize the cast list has become unmanageable, and you need to downsize a little.

In this session, the goal is to identify and eliminate unnecessary characters.

Step One: Write Down Your Protagonist and Antagonist

Take a sheet of paper (or do this on a screen) and draw two boxes in the middle, evenly spaced apart. Write your protagonist's name in one box, your antagonist's name in the other. Add boxes if you have more than one of either. If you find yourself adding a *lot* of boxes, that's a problem.

Step Two: Add the Other Characters in the Novel

Start adding boxes with the other characters' names in them. Put them below the protagonist if they're directly connected to her, above the antagonist if they're connected to him. To quickly see what level of importance they are, try using different colors per level. List in order:

- Major secondary characters first (friends, sidekicks)
- Important characters (people the plot or story hinges on, but who aren't hanging out with the main characters)
- Minor characters (recurring people who play smaller roles and are seen multiple times)
- Named walk-on characters (people in one or two scenes who don't do much, but have names anyway)
- Any remaining people who interact with your protagonist or antagonist, named or not

For this exercise, let's say a "character" is anyone who is: A) named, as names = importance to a reader and suggest they should be remembered, or B) shown on the page affecting the protagonist (or antagonist). "People" are those who are unnamed, but interact with the main characters. For example, if your protagonist is mugged by three thugs, there are four "bodies" in that scene—one character and three people.

Do this for all the characters and people in your novel.

Step Three: Connect the Characters

Draw lines connecting the boxes. Use a solid line if the character directly interacts with and affects the protagonist, a dotted line if they're connected to someone who is connected to the protagonist. For example, when the protagonist is mugged by three thugs, and only one speaks to her and interacts in a meaningful way, that thug gets a solid connection line. The other two thugs would get dotted lines to the first thug, because they're connected to *him*, but don't directly interact with the protagonist.

What This Should Tell You:

- How many characters are in the book
- Which characters directly affect your protagonist and which don't
- Which characters might be good candidates to cut or combine

🚩 **REVISION RED FLAG:** If you had a hard time finding room for all your boxes, you probably have too many characters. Same if you have a lot of characters who have zero connections to your protagonist, but connections to other characters in the book. Lots of people with dotted lines to one person could be combined into one or two people who fill multiple or similar roles.

This exercise is also useful to see if a particular scene has too many characters in it, especially those hard-to-manage scenes with a group of people all chiming in about something. Look at who matters in that scene and who is there to toss out a single comment.

This exercise forces you to examine the connections between characters. You might think a character is affecting the protagonist, but when you sit down and *really* look at it, he has no direct interaction with her at all. He's more connected to someone who is connected to the protagonist.

Sometimes a visual representation can provide more information than a list, and looking at your stories from a different perspective can allow you to see connections you normally would have missed.

If you discover you *do* have too many characters, you have several options for wrangling them into a manageable number:

Option One: Get Rid of Characters You Don't Need

Deleting characters is by far the easiest way to reduce your cast, though sometimes the most painful option if you're attached to them. Look back at your boxes, or make a list of every character in the novel, starting with the main characters, and move down to the minor named walk-ons.

Who doesn't *need* to be there? Maybe one of the minor named walk-ons can become "the server" instead of Maria the waitress, or the conversation in the diner can be moved to a new setting where another person isn't needed.

Determine what would change if you cut that character. Would it create a problem or would a minor edit here and there fix his absence? If his departure has little to no bearing on the book, go ahead and say goodbye.

Option Two: Show Clingy Characters the Door

The longer a story is, the more likely it is to accumulate extra characters. This happens often in series, where characters with past roles stick around long after they've done their jobs. Story logic says they'd be in a particular scene, but there's no graceful way to get them into the story. They're in the way and might even hijack the plot if you try to give them more to do to justify them being there.

Find the characters who are in the scene only because it feels like they *have* to be. There's a decent chance these characters irritate you, because you know they're mucking the scene up and you're trying to shove them in—such as, the protagonist wouldn't cast off his faithful servant, but he's too much of a hassle to deal with if he's always around.

Look for ways to remove this type of character from the story in a plausible way. Think about why the protagonist *wouldn't* want that servant around. You might even be able to add conflict with his removal, as the heartbroken hero is forced to send her beloved friend away for his own safety.

Option Three: Let an Existing Character Do the Work Instead

Another easy fix is to let an existing character do the job instead of giving it to a new character. Look at your smaller walk-on roles, which can often be fleshed out to include the new tasks needed for the story. If the walk-on won't work, perhaps a more important character can do that task or exhibit that skill, or cause the problem. Instead of adding a character, add a layer to someone already there.

Often, the who doesn't matter as much as the what, and a character is there to do a specific job. If the reasons for a character being in that scene (or book) are general (and not specific to that character), you can likely accomplish the same thing by using an existing character.

Option Four: Reconnect a Smaller Character to the Bigger Picture or Problem

Sometimes you have characters you want to use, but they don't do all that much. You have *reasons* for wanting them in there (often dealing with backstory or world building), but their presence causes more problems than it solves. They feel unconnected to the story because they're unconnected to the plot, and thus stand out. If you give them more to do, they might not feel so useless or extraneous.

With a little creative thinking, they might be able to help solve *other* problems, such as a world-building issue or a plot hole. Maybe give them a history or skill that allows you to show an aspect of the world, or connect them to the protagonist's past to show a critical piece of her history. They could be the missing piece of a puzzle that isn't quite fitting into another part of the manuscript.

Option Five: Check for Unnecessary Subplots

A large cast can be a red flag for a bloated plot, so it's not a bad idea to check the subplots for any extra characters. Kill a subplot and every unique character in that subplot can also go. Not only do you cut down the cast, you eliminate a subplot that was probably bogging down the story anyway.

Streamlining a too-large cast can be tough, but you'll have a much tighter (and better) story once you cut away the dead weight.

If You Want to Flesh Out the Characters

Unless you did little to no character development before you started writing (which is possible), you have at least a basic sense of who your characters are. After all, you needed to know *something* about them in order to write them, even if they still need some work.

In this session, the goal is to further develop any weak characters.

Your character arc analysis will come in handy here, since you'll have a guide on how (and where) your characters need to grow to complete their arcs. Look for any notes on weak or underdeveloped characters and begin with them. You might also take a peek at any scenes with weak goals or motivations—a weak character could be the reason, since you don't know them well enough to know what they'd want in that scene.

Step One: Evaluate the Character's Role

Before you start adding character details, consider what role that character plays and how she affects the novel as a whole. This can help determine the best way to flesh out the character for your novel. You don't want to throw in random "stuff" that does nothing to improve the story, but add the right details to deepen a character in a way that best serves the story.

Explore what the character did: Look at what the character did in the novel (actions, choices, mistakes, goals, issues, etc.) and think about what shaped her to be the person who acted that way or made those decisions.

Explore why the character did it: Look at the motivations behind the actions and add reasons or history as to why those choices were made.

Explore the character's mistakes: Look at any mistakes or bad choices the character made in the novel and work backward to add a flaw that could have contributed to them.

Explore the character's victories: Look for any victories or successes and add positive traits that would logically have helped the character in those moments.

Explore the character's views and beliefs: Look for what the character believes or how she sees the world or events in the novel, and add traits (positive and negative) that helped shape those views.

If you want additional questions to help develop a flat or weak character, look at these specific areas (pick as many or as few as you need). Adapt or adjust these questions to suit your own story:

Personality and Voice

Personality influences how a character will interact with the other characters in the novel. Characters *can* have inconsistencies, but, typically, personality traits blend and support each other, and are based on a character's history and upbringing.

What kind of person is she? If you were describing her to a friend, how would you do it? This helps identify how you see this character.

How does she answer questions? This helps identify how open or forthcoming she is.

How does she present herself to other people? This helps identify how she wants others to see her.

Is her outer voice different from her inner voice? How? Why? This helps identify how much she's concealing about her own feelings.

Which personality traits help her? Which hurt her? This helps identify where her flaws and virtues lie.

How did she get that way? This helps identify the important aspects of her backstory.

How organized is she? This helps identify how she approaches problems.

Does she plan or react? This helps identify how cautious or impulsive she is.

Can she be depended on? This helps identify how connected she is to others, and how trustworthy she is.

Is she outgoing or reserved? This helps identify where she falls on the introvert/extrovert scale, and how she approaches situations.

How compassionate is she? This helps identify how she relates to and empathizes with others.

Is she willing to work with others? This helps identify how controlling or accepting she is.

Is she inherently trusting of people she doesn't know? This helps identify what's hurt her in the past.

Is she helpful or does she worry about herself first? This helps identify how selfish she is.

How excitable is she? This helps identify how she reacts in intense or emotional situations.

How confident is she? This helps identify how strongly she pursues her goals.

How does she handle the unexpected? This helps identify how she reacts to surprises.

How emotional is she overall? This helps identify her general emotional state.

Needs and Wants

What a character needs and wants will determine the goals and motivations for the plot. The character's personality will determine how he goes about getting those needs and wants.

What are his critical needs? This helps identify what's influencing the character's decisions. Look for needs that will help your plot unfold.

How self-motivated is he to act? This helps identify whether or not he'll act on his own or if he requires an outside push.

How much effort will he exert to achieve a goal? This helps identify the types of solutions to plot problems. Will he take the easy way out or do what's right even if it's hard?

How ambitious is he? This helps identify how hard he'll fight to win and what levels he'll strive for.

How assertive is he? This helps identify how direct he is in trying to achieve his goal.

How positive is he? This helps identify his outlook on life.

Does he want to do things on his terms or just follow along? This helps identify how well he works with others.

Hopes and Dreams

A character's hopes and dreams determine the character arc and often connect directly to the internal conflict. These are usually the things she feels she'll never have, but needs to be happy.

What are her hopes, both in general and in the specific story problem? This helps identify her character arc and what she wants from life.

What does she dream about? This helps identify unconscious needs she doesn't feel she deserves.

If she wasn't dealing with the problems of the novel, what would she be doing? This helps identify if she's being oppressed or held back by the story events or elements.

Flaws and Fears

A character's flaws and fears help create conflict in the novel, providing reasons for him to make mistakes and do the wrong things.

What are his flaws? This helps identify places for him to grow as a character, and areas he might make mistakes in.

What does he fear? This helps identify potential areas he can use as excuses or reasons that can cause him to make the wrong decision.

What are his prejudices? This helps identify where he's ignorant or misguided. Prejudices are useful when you need your protagonist to instantly dislike another character for plot reasons and he has no good reason to do so.

What makes him uncomfortable? This helps identify fears and concerns, as well as judge where his moral compass lies.

What makes him furious beyond rational thought? This helps identify what he feels strongly about.

What makes him change the subject or walk away from a conversation? This helps identify his bli

nd spots, or what he's trying to avoid.

Strengths and Weaknesses

A character's strengths typically drive the plot, while her weaknesses drive the character arc.

What are her strengths? This helps identify the positive skills she might use to complete the novel's tasks.

What do you admire about her? This helps identify admirable or redeeming aspects.

What are her weaknesses? This helps identify where she still needs to grow as a person.

What causes her problems? This helps identify common mistakes and flaws.

What are the negative aspects about her personality? This helps identify traits that can get her into trouble.

How does she handle stress? This helps identify how well she'll handle the pressures of the plot.

Views and Opinions

Readers see a story world through a character's eyes. What he sees, they see, what he believes, they believe. These opinions and worldviews form his personality and give him a foundation for his flaws and virtues.

How does he feel about the world around him? This helps identify how he views the world he lives in.

How does he feel about the other characters? This helps identify possible personal conflicts.

How does he feel about the problem at hand? This helps identify how he'll approach resolving the problem.

What doesn't he want to think about? This helps identify what he's trying to avoid.

Does he question the world around him? This helps identify how accepting he is of the status quo.

Does he want to know why, even if the reason is hard to understand or even find? This helps identify how curious he is, and how willing he might be to push for answers.

Does he accept the way things are or what people tell him? This helps identify how trusting he is.

Likes and Dislikes

What a character likes and dislikes makes her feel real to readers and shows her human side.

What makes her happy? This helps identify possible motivations to act.

What makes her sad? This helps identify possible stakes.

What pisses her off? This helps identify ways to cause her to react irrationally.

Ethics and Morality

What a character considers right or wrong changes based on the world he lives in. It's his job as a character to show readers the ethics of the story world.

What are his morals and religious background? This helps identify where his morality might fall, and where his intolerances are.

What does he think is fair? Unfair? This helps identify his sense of justice and what he's willing to accept from others.

Background and Family

Family can have significant influence on who a character is and what she'll do.

Where did she grow up? This helps identify any cultural morals and views.

What was her childhood like? This helps identify how she relates to and interacts with others.

What was the most traumatic thing to ever happen to her? This helps identify deep emotional influences on her behavior.

What was the best thing to ever happen to her? This helps identify positive influences on her, or shed insights into her hopes and dreams.

How did these two events shape her perceptions of the world? This helps identify how she approaches and solves problems.

Who is her family? This helps identify how she handles relationships.

What was her economic background? This helps identify how she values money and wealth, and what importance she places on it.

What was her educational background? This helps identify where her knowledge (or lack thereof) comes from.

What are the key defining moments in her past, both good and bad? This helps identify the events with the most influence on her behavior and decision-making skills.

Friends and Enemies

You can tell a lot about a person by who his friends (and enemies) are. We naturally seek out people with similar views to our own.

Who are his friends? This helps identify different aspects of his personality, and the type of person he is. It also could be a pool of allies to draw from.

Who are his enemies? This helps identify potential antagonists or troublemakers, as well as aspects of his personality he dislikes.

What won't he do to help another character? This helps identify how far he's willing to go, or what lines he won't cross.

What does he like about his friends? Dislike about them? This helps identify his values and what he wants and expects from people. Are they allies or tools?

How large is his circle of friends? This helps identify how likable or outgoing he is.

What types of social situations is he comfortable with? This helps identify how he'll react when faced with the plot's problems.

Is he energized or drained by people? This helps identify how well he works in a group, or if he prefers to work alone.

How are his relationships with other characters? This helps identify potential conflicts, and places for growth.

How easily does he make new friends or allies? This helps identify how hard it is for him to gain allies or help for his problem.

Roles and Obligations

Some characters are created to fill a particular role or show a perspective different from the protagonist's.

What role does she play? This helps identify how she fits thematically and how much she might have to do.

Does she see herself in this role, or does she play it unconsciously? This helps identify how committed to the role she is, or if she's being manipulated.

How do others see her? This helps identify if she's true to herself or changes to suit what others expect of her.

How does she feel about how others see her? This helps identify her level of self confidence.

Characters are both predictable and unpredictable at the same time. Their past can show insights into their behaviors, but their personal quirks and idiosyncrasies mean that they won't always act as expected or be who you expect them to be.

Now that you've worked out what's inside your characters, let's focus a little on the outsides.

If You Want to Adjust the Character Descriptions

There's no rule on how much you need to describe your characters. Some writers will toss out a detail here and there and call it done, while others will give enough details to create an accurate police sketch.

In this session, the goal is to determine the right level of detail, and make sure your character descriptions are serving your story, not bogging it down.

Step One: Make Sure *You* Know What Your Characters Look Like

This might seem like a ridiculous step, but not everyone thinks about what a character looks like on a first draft (I don't, for example). Some writers focus more on figuring out who a character is than what she looks like, and often don't decide on physical details until the second draft.

Look at your character list. For every character who doesn't have the standard police-blotter description (and needs one), go ahead and create it (unless of course, you aren't using physical descriptions in your novel).

This is also a good time to flesh out or create your story bible to keep track of these kinds of details. It's not uncommon to forget what color eyes a secondary character has, or where someone grew up. This is especially useful if you plan to write more than one book with these characters.

Step Two: Add or Strengthen Descriptions When a Character is Introduced

The first time readers meet a character is typically when she's described. For point-of-view characters, these details are often spread out over the scene or chapter. For non-point-of-view characters, it's common to see the details in a quick summary from the point-of-view character in that scene.

The more details you add, the more you'll want to keep it in your point-of-view character's head. Let *her* judge what she's seeing so the details do more than just describe. They'll also characterize and do some world building at the same time.

When fleshing out the descriptions, consider:

What are the obvious physical details about the character? The classic hair, eye, height, etc., details.

What are details that only the point-of-view character would notice? Describe anything that gives you an opportunity to share a little insight into the point-of-view character. What does *she* see and how does she feel about it?

What details suggest or hint at what's unique about that particular character? If the character is a world-class pianist, maybe the point-of-view character notices long, graceful fingers. If he's ex-special forces, then maybe there's a scar or military bearing that stands out.

Readers remember what they see first, so pick the critical details you want associated with the character.

Step Three: Revise Any Clichéd or Stereotypical Descriptions

Clichés and stereotypes are information shorthand, so they slip into first drafts all the time. Go through your scenes and rework any descriptions that rely on clichés or stereotypes.

Some common clichés to look for:

Characters describing themselves in a mirror: Unless you've come up with a unique way to have the character look in a mirror (or any reflective surface) and describe themselves, look for other ways to show the description.

Characters introducing themselves to readers: Another common cliché is to have the character introduce themselves and then say what they look like. "I'm your average gal, five foot four, brown hair, blue eyes," or, "I'm nothing special, six foot, black cropped hair and brown almond eyes."

Characters slipping in a detail: It's not bad to see a detail slipped in casually, but it can read awkwardly depending on the narrative distance. For example, "I brushed my long, blond hair" can sound too self-aware. Who remarks on the length and color of their hair when they brush it?

Overdone physical traits: There's a bit of a joke in young adult fiction that a large percentage of best friends have red hair (and yes, I'm guilty of it, too). Villains are often dark haired with dark eyes, while sweet, innocent characters are blond and pale, and funny sidekicks are brunettes with quirks. It's not a bad idea to look at your descriptions and think about *why* you chose them. Are you inadvertently using a stereotype or cliché?

Characters with stereotypical defining details: Be wary of having one particular detail that defines a character in a stereotypical way. Not all Asians are martial arts experts, not all southerners are slow, and not all Christians are Bible thumpers.

Yes, people *can* be stereotypes in real life, but it's the writer's job to find a fresher, more original way to portray the characters.

Step Four: Trim Any Extraneous Character Description

Not every writer will need to add description—some will have too much and will want to do a little trimming. Trust your instincts on this, and if it feels like too much, cut back a little.

If you're not sure what can go, cut back wherever you use more than three details in a row. If you notice you use multiple details a lot, try reducing them by half and see how it reads. Add more details as needed.

At this stage, you've strengthened who your characters are and what they look like. Next, let's work on what they want out of life (and this novel).

If You Want to Strengthen the Character Arc

At the heart of every character arc is the internal conflict. Your characters feel conflicted, and that emotional struggle is preventing them from getting what they want and being who they want to be. The goal of the character arc is to put them through the grinder so they learn the lessons necessary to become the people they feel like inside. No matter how much or how little the protagonist arcs, the internal conflict will drive her and affect her choices in the novel.

In this session, the goal is to develop any weak internal conflicts to create stronger character arcs.

Step One: Examine the Internal Conflict

The internal conflict is the problem the protagonist is facing on the inside. It's often a personal struggle that deals with the protagonist's belief system—something she values, something she was taught, something she "knows" is true.

What is keeping your protagonist from being happy or feeling satisfied? What's the one thing she needs to feel fulfilled? Unlike the external goals, this goal can be vague or even something the character isn't aware of yet, such as: the need to feel safe, though she doesn't yet know where her unease is coming from.

What's the internal problem your protagonist is facing? This is usually due to personal self-doubt, uncertainty, or a flaw she has to overcome. It often relates to the external plot issue, such as: The protagonist's goal is to move overseas for a new job, but she has a fear of flying.

How is this inner problem forcing your protagonist to make an impossible choice? This can help determine the major character growth points—the moments where the internal forces act on the external in a big way.

How does this inner problem directly oppose the external problems? The inner problem or flaw usually causes the character to make mistakes. For example, if the problem is trusting others, it could result in the protagonist not heeding the advice that will help her at a crucial moment. Letting the inner problem negatively influence the protagonist at key moments can turn weak scenes into strong, high-stakes scenes.

 REVISION RED FLAG: If the protagonist has no internal conflict, that could indicate a lack of stakes or personal motivations for her to act in the novel. There should be pros and cons to every choice she faces, usually driven by this internal issue. If this is weak or missing, consider doing the exercises in If You Want to Flesh Out the Characters on page 70 to determine what drives the character, or try the exercises in *Book Two: Fixing Your Plot and Story Structure Problems* to strengthen the backstory, goals, conflicts, stakes, and/or motivations.

Step Two: Determine the Beginning and End of the Character's Arc

Once you're clear on where the internal conflict lies, focus on how you see that character evolving over the course of the novel.

Where does the character end up? A strong arc will show the lessons learned or flaws overcome during the novel. Look for how the character becomes a different person (for better or for worse) by the end of the book. Identify the personal changes, and what caused those changes. Look for the moments in the novel where these changes occur to see where the arc advances.

How much does the character need to suffer to achieve this change? Nobody changes for the fun of it. A good character arc will make the character reevaluate her behavior and realize she needs to make a change or else. If the character is going to evolve in a major way, the events that force that change will be equally major. Look for the moments or triggers that force these changes.

Who or what brings about that change? The character usually exhibits the behavior that needs changing and it turns out badly for her early on in the novel. Eventually, she'll behave the right way and be rewarded. Typically, this takes many small steps in a longer process to make the character take a hard look at herself and her life. Identify the clear path (even if there are setbacks) between the beginning and the end of the novel.

How does the change reflect the premise or theme? Odds are the arc is going to connect to the theme or premise, since character growth is a common vehicle for illustrating theme. Look at what the story is about on a more conceptual level, and if the character arc can help illustrate that idea. Pinpoint where the character arc illustrates the theme.

🚩 **REVISION RED FLAG:** If you have trouble identifying or answering these questions, that could indicate where the weak links in the character arc fall. How and why a character changes are the two most common areas of weakness.

Step Three: Check That the Character Arc is Arcing

Once you've identified all the right arc points, verify that they're unfolding in the right places throughout the novel. Refer back to your character arc map and fill in any missing or weak spots. Some variation is normal, so if the arc is unfolding over the entire novel at a good pace, you don't have to hit every single point exactly as stated. These are guidelines, not rules.

Identify where the protagonist's flaw is established: This is usually seen in the opening scene or first few chapters. If not, look for ways to add an example of the flaw in this area.

Identify where the protagonist makes her first mistake: This usually happens on or around the inciting event, and might even cause the event. If the protagonist makes no mistake, look for ways to add that to this area.

Identify where the attempt to grow fails: The first attempt to change usually doesn't go well, and is often seen around the end of Act One when the plot problems start putting pressure on the protagonist. If there's no growth attempt, or the attempt to grow fails, look for ways to add the attempt or have attempt to grow not turn out as expected. Show the character trying and failing to be a better person.

Identify where the protagonist is blindsided by weakness: It's common for the flaw or weakness to cause unexpected failure, often around the midpoint of the novel. Is there a moment when the character is surprised or caught off guard because of her flaw? If not, look for ways to create something unexpected (good or bad) around the midpoint.

Identify where there's a major screw-up or rejection of growth: This usually triggers the classic Dark Moment of the Soul just before the climax (Act Three) starts, and is the personal demon the protagonist must face in order to move forward. If you have no moment of despair, look for ways the character's flaw might emotionally destroy her right before she needs to be her strongest.

Identify where the protagonist realizes she's grown: This is the culmination of everything she's learned and experienced over the course of the novel, and the result of the soul searching she did during her dark moment. If there is no realization, look for ways the character arc can influence and aid (or hurt if it's that kind of novel) how the climax unfolds.

> **REVISION RED FLAG:** If you have trouble identifying or answering these questions, that could indicate the arc isn't arcing. Consider returning to your character arc map and adjusting where the arc moments occur in the novel.

Step Four: Overlay the Character Arc With the Plot Arc

The ebb and flow between the external and internal conflicts helps control the pacing and narrative drive of the novel. Examining how the two sides interact can reveal structure or pacing problems.

- A traditional dual-conflict arc has these common turning points:
- Establishing the protagonist's flaw occurs on or around the opening scene
- Protagonist's first mistake occurs on or around the inciting event
- Attempt to grow fails occurs on or around the end of Act One (Act One problem)
- Blindsided by weakness occurs on or around the midpoint reversal
- Major screw-up or rejection of growth occurs on or around the end of Act Two (Act Two disaster, the All is Lost moment, the Dark Night of the Soul)
- Realization of growth occurs on or around the climax

> **REVISION RED FLAG:** If these moments are way off, or the character arc has no bearing on the plot arc, that could indicate the internal conflict isn't working with the external plot arc. Consider focusing on how the two conflicts (internal and external) relate to and affect each

other so they work together to bring about the character's change. If they mostly line up and it feels right, it's likely working as intended.

While you don't have to stick to this basic structure, it's a proven way to see how the inner conflict and character growth can aid with plotting and increase the tension and conflict for the entire story. Adjust as needed, but if you want a little extra guidance, this format will give you a solid structure to work with.

You should now have strong, well-developed characters with solid character arcs, so let's take a moment to see how they became that way.

If You Want to Balance the Backstory

Everybody has a backstory. In fiction though, that past isn't always relevant, even if it *is* interesting. Readers like to see a story moving, and stopping to explain a character's history tends to bog down the narrative. Too much backstory is high on the list of why agents reject a manuscript, and many advise to cut all backstory from the first fifty pages. This is why it's critical to find the right backstory balance.

In this session, the goal is to eliminate any unnecessary backstory and find the right balance for your novel.

If you made notes in your editorial or character arc maps on scenes with too much backstory (or not enough), start with those.

Step One: Eliminate Unnecessary Backstory

Once you've identified any unnecessary backstory for a scene, you have three choices—cut it, move it to where it *is* relevant, or make it relevant in that scene. Your character arc map can show the most relevant aspects of the character's personality, and guide you in gauging the backstory needed.

If you're unsure if the backstory is unnecessary, consider:

How does it affect the scene's goal? Backstory that affects motivation seems natural because it has a place in the story. If the backstory has no bearing on what the protagonist is trying to do in that scene, either directly or by affecting a decision made in that scene, then it's probably not needed.

Were any of the scene's characters involved in the backstory? If the backstory changes the way readers (or even characters) see the scene, it might be worth keeping. Unless of course, that change steals tension or reveals a secret better left a mystery.

How does the point-of-view character feel about the backstory? People think about the past when it has relevance to the present. If the point-of-view character doesn't care, or isn't affected by the backstory, there's no need to reveal it.

Step Two: Revise Backstory to Show, Not Tell

Take a look at the remaining backstory and ask: Is it showing or telling the information? Backstory is a common place for told prose to sneak in as you explain the history and why it matters to the character at that time.

🚩 **REVISION RED FLAG:** Look for common telling words, such as "in order to" or "because" or "which" or "once" to help spot backstory. If you're stopping the story to explain something, it's telling, not showing.

Revision Option: Ways to Hide the Backstory

If you have backstory that needs to be there, try slipping it into the text in small bites, or disguise it as something else.

Background the backstory: Hiding the backstory in plain sight is a handy trick to get the information into the story without stopping the story to explain it. For example, if you wanted to tell readers about the terrible past of your protagonist, and that she spent nine years in an underground prison, consider how might she might behave *because of* that experience. Is she extra sensitive to the light? Claustrophobic? Skilled at getting around when she can't see well? By putting your backstory in the background (backgrounding), you can flesh out your characters and show their history without stopping the story to explain it. Better still, you'll leave enough tantalizing hints that readers eventually *want* to know the whole story.

Drop teasing hints: Instead of revealing all of a character's past, try dropping hints here and there to tease readers into *wanting* to know the history. Look for places to toss in a casual comment or exhibit an interesting skill that's never explained. After a while, readers will be so intrigued they'll have no problem with the story pausing while this history is explained in more depth.

🚩 **REVISION RED FLAG:** Be wary of being *too* vague with hints and clues. Find the right balance between a tease and being too cryptic to be understood, which can turn readers off and confuse them. Make readers think, "Oooh, what's *that* all about?" not "What the heck are they talking about?"

Revision Option: If You Need More Backstory, Not Less

There *are* rare instances when a novel needs *more* backstory, so if analyzing your backstory reveals certain scenes require additional information to be fully understood, go ahead and flesh out those details. Just make sure what's being added is truly necessary.

Red flags that a scene needs more backstory include:

Readers are having a hard time understanding the importance of the scene: If your beta readers or critique partners aren't catching the significance of a scene, or don't know why something matters, you might need a little backstory to explain the motives or significance.

The critical information has never been discussed or shown: While most of a character's past can be shown in how she interacts with the world, sometimes the only way to convey that information is by telling the backstory of that character.

The backstory is complicated: In genre novels with a lot of world building, it's more common to see an above-average amount of backstory. It's much harder to glean clues from how a character acts when the world isn't a world readers are familiar with.

Backstory isn't just explaining the characters' history; it's showing the experiences that shaped their lives and made them act the way they do.

You want to mention what's *driving* characters to act, not just events that happened in their pasts. Pick what's important both to the character and to the story itself.

After doing all this character work, the final step is to connect it all and give it greater meaning through your theme.

If You Want to Develop the Theme

If plot is a novel's skeleton, and characters are the muscle, then theme is its soul. It's what the book is *about*, and without it, a story can feel shallow at best, pointless at worst. Themes keep readers thinking about your novel long after they've put it down.

In this session, the goal is to look at your themes and see how they can guide you to a stronger story.

Step One: Strengthen the Theme(s)

Go through your editorial map and look for examples that reflect your theme.

Are there any weak scenes that could be improved by adding a thematic layer? Look for any decision-making scenes, scenes where the characters face a consequence for their actions, or scenes involving a moral or ethical dilemma.

Do thematic scenes coincide with major plot points and character growth moments? Not every turning point needs to reflect the theme, but if none do, that's a red flag the theme doesn't truly affect the story.

Are any of the scenes a stretch to fit the theme? If so, clarify how and why that scene reflects the theme.

Step Two: Eliminate Competing or Conflicting Themes

For every story that has no theme, you'll find one with too many themes. While you can have more than one theme (story themes plus character themes), if you find yourself with a long list of what the novel is about thematically, it's probably trying to do too much and not giving any one concept the attention it deserves.

A general rule of thumb: aim for no more than one theme for the story itself, and one theme per major character. If those character themes can fall under the story theme, so much the better. For example, if the story theme is "justice," then character themes might be, "Where's the line between justice and revenge?" or, "How far will you go for a loved one?"

Also be on the lookout for any themes that conflict. If the story theme is, "Love conquers all" and the protagonist's personal theme is, "You can't fight city hall," that could pose problems identifying what the story is about. Should they fight or not?

Step Three: Use Your Theme to Guide Your Revision

Theme can help you decide what details you want to use, and what ideas you want to show. For example, if you're fleshing out your setting, you can use details that show the world and also convey the theme. If the protagonist is looking for justice, you might show examples of the injustice of that world and why this is a noble pursuit. Or you might show examples of other people finding justice to illustrate why the protagonist needs it so badly. If love is the theme, there might be red roses, or hearts, or other details that suggest love scattered about.

Revision Option: Adding a Theme

If you don't have a theme and would like to add one, start by examining what you already have in the novel. There's a good chance you have a theme lurking in there that needs drawing out. Ask yourself:

What larger concepts did you explore with your novel? Theme is often found in the conceptual level of your story.

If you had to pick one cliché or adage to describe your novel, what would it be? Clichés capture a thematic concept and show a larger idea with just a few words.

What are common problems in your novel? Do they point to a theme? Look at the various issues your characters are facing. The types of problems they face often point to a common theme.

What are common character flaws or dreams? Themes are frequently found in what the protagonist wants or dreams about, or even what she wishes she could overcome.

Themes can connect every aspect of your novel and tie the characters and the plot together. Now that the first half of your manuscript (your characters) is strong, let's move on to developing your point of view

Workshop Three: Point of View Work

The Goal of This Workshop: To strengthen the point of view and internalization of your manuscript.

What We'll Discuss in This Workshop: How to analyze your manuscript for common point of view and narrator errors, and find ways to strengthen the point of view and internalization.

Welcome to Workshop Three: Point of View Work

Readers will experience your novel by seeing the story through the point-of-view character's eyes. Your point-of-view characters are their guides to what happens, conveying the information readers need to know (and hiding it when necessary) so they feel part of the story. It's the most powerful tool in your writer toolbox, allowing you to show how your characters feel, think, see, and judge the situations you put them in.

A strong point of view also guides you as a writer and helps you determine the right details for your story, and the right way to add those details to the scene.

Analyze the Point of View

Weak points of view hurt a novel, because readers have no sense of who's telling the story. Scenes can seem detached, aimless, even dry with nothing but generic descriptions and explanations that "tell" a story, but don't allow a reader to experience that story.

In this session, the goal is to examine your point of view for common problems.

Point of view and internalization are closely linked, so you'll examine how that's working next.

Step One: Determine if the Narrator is Working

The narrator tells the story, whether she's a character in the novel with a tight first person point of view, or a distant omniscient third-person point of view outside the story.

Go through the following questions to clarify who your narrator is and how she's working with your novel:

- **Is it clear who the narrator is?** Even in a first-person point of view, reminding yourself who is telling the tale can be a good thing. It's a nudge to remember to put the narrative in *her* voice, use *her* judgment, *her* worldview, and not yours.
- **Is the narrator's voice consistent with the novel's tone?** Maybe the narrator is flippant and sarcastic, or reverent and respectful. Whatever she is, this voice will permeate the entire novel, so you'll want it to fit the story's tone.
- **Is the narrator getting in the way of the story?** Some narrators simply narrate, but others play a role and influence events. Where does your narrator fall on that scale?
- **Is the narrator revealing too much? Not enough?** Fully omniscient narrators know and see all, but the less all-knowing narrator might not be privy to everything that happens in a novel. A retrospective narrator might only know what was told to her or what she personally witnessed.

No matter what story you're telling, *somebody* is behind it. Understanding who that person is can help you create a richer novel that better illustrates the story you want to share.

Step Two: Determine if the Point of View is Working

Point-of-view errors can make a novel seem distant, confusing, or even awkward. Go through the following questions and determine if there are any point-of-view issues:

- **Are there any point-of-view shifts?** Look for places where the point of view is suddenly out of a non-point-of-view character's eyes, or revealing information the point-of-view character couldn't know.
- **Is the point of view consistent?** Are there any scenes in a point-of-view style that differs from the rest of the manuscript? This could indicate a scene that's there to dump information or explain something about the story.
- **Is there too much filtering?** Filter words distance readers from the point-of-view character, remind them they're reading, explain details that are obvious, and often lead you into telling or crafting passive sentences. Look for words such as heard, felt, thought, saw, etc.
- **Do characters know details they couldn't possibly know?** Look for places where characters sound like mind readers and know what the other characters are thinking, and places where characters make huge leaps in logic without any groundwork for it.
- **Are any point-of-view characters oddly self-aware?** People don't typically self-analyze their motives and reasons for acting. Be wary of characters who know why (and state why) they're feeling or acting during a highly emotional state.
- **Are there any inconsistent or out-of-the-blue emotional responses?** Look for reactions where characters overreact, suggesting they know more than what made it to the page.
- **Are any point-of-view characters stating the obvious?** Look for places where the characters are explaining what is clear by how they're acting.

- **Are any point-of-view characters reacting before something happens?** This could indicate that the stimulus/response structure is off, which could confuse readers.
- **Are there any point-of-view scenes that are there only to show information the main characters can't witness?** If so, you're better off finding another way for your characters to discover that information.
- **Do you use one point of view per scene (if it's not an omniscient point of view)?** If not, you might be shifting points of view within a scene.
- **Is it clear when you've switched points of view?** Make sure you give readers a clue when you change point-of-view characters. Use a name in the opening paragraph, or some other indicator of whose head you're in.

REVISION RED FLAG: It's not uncommon to have a lot of unnecessary points of view in a first draft as you explore the story and determine the best way to tell it. Watch out for characters with only one or two scenes—they might be there just to dump information. Another common issue to watch out for is a single-point-of-view character who relays every aspect of their day.

Problems Found?

If you find any point-of-view issues, spend some time doing the exercises in If You Want to Strengthen Your Point of View on page 98.

Analyze the Internalization

Internalization is the window into the minds of your point-of-view characters. It lets you know what they think and how they feel, which helps you craft a compelling narrative flow that hooks readers and makes them care about the characters.

In this session, the goal is to examine your internalization for potential problems.

Determine if the Internalization is Working

It can be challenging to find the right balance of internalization and action, and many first drafts go too far in one direction or the other (too much or too little).

- **Is there too much internalization?** Too much thinking is often seen in slow areas, or places when the pacing drags. It could also indicate a protagonist who's thinking more than acting.
- **Is there too little internalization?** Not enough thinking can indicate a lack of motivation or goals, or the understanding of those goals. Readers don't know why characters are acting or what it means. Sometimes, you don't know either, which is why the internalization is light.
- **Does the internal thought clarify the dialogue or action?** Good internalization works with dialogue and action to show why and how a character is acting. Look for any places where the thoughts muddy or confuse what's going on.
- **Does the internal thought show the point-of-view character's opinion on the situation?** Who the character is shows in how she thinks and what she thinks about. Look for places where the thoughts are flat and devoid of personality.
- **Does the internal thought provide necessary information without infodumping?** Characters think about what matters to them; they don't dump unnecessary details into the story. Look for scenes where characters explain a lot of information or the text reads more like the author making notes. Keep an eye out for details you think are "necessary" that are infodumps in disguise.
- **Does the internal thought convey background information without telling**? Internal thoughts should imply details of the character's backstory, not stop the story to explain those details or why they matter. Look for places where characters suddenly sound like they're reading from someone's dossier, a travel guide, or a textbook.
- **Are there internal thoughts in *every* line of dialogue?** Too much thinking bogs a story down. Be wary of scenes where the character mentally debates something every time she speaks.

- Are the internal thoughts often paragraphs long, and do they happen every time the point-of-view character thinks? This is a red flag for protagonists who think too much, and often act too little.
- Does the internal thought summarize a scene or idea at the end (or describe it at the start before you show that scene or idea)? Be wary of thoughts that summarize the action of the scene. Often, the thoughts tell readers what's about to happen and lessen the tension.
- Are you repeating the same idea in multiple ways? Sometimes you show the same thing through thought and action, such as having the character slam the door, scream, "I hate him!" and then think, *She was so pissed.* The screaming and dialogue make it clear how the character feels.

🚩 **REVISION RED FLAG:** Internalization is a common area to find infodumps (both description and backstory) and told prose. If you've gotten feedback about those issues, try checking your internalization for trouble.

Problems Found?

If you find any internalization issues, spend some time doing the exercises in If You Want to Streamline the Internalization on page 102.

If You Want to Strengthen the Point of View

A strong point of view leads to a strong novel. It helps you decide what details to use when describing, allows you to show how the world works and what the rules of the world are, and it lets your characters show your readers that world.

In this session, the goal is to fix common point-of-view problems.

Step One: Revise Any Unnecessary Filtering

A point-of-view character, by definition, is relaying (and thus filtering) everything she sees, hears, feels, touches, smells, thinks. If it's described, readers know she experienced it.

Depending on your narrative distance, different degrees of filtering are acceptable and even expected. Sometimes this filter is invisible and readers don't feel any distance between them and the point-of-view character. Other times the filters are obvious and readers feel the wall between them and the characters. One looks *through* the eyes of the point-of-view character, the other looks *at* the point-of-view character.

General rule of thumb: The tighter the point of view, the less filtering you usually see.

Filter words typically show up in told prose, passive prose, or weak writing. You'll also find them in unintentionally distant points of view.

Common red flag filter words: Saw, heard, felt, knew, watched, decided, noticed, realized, wondered, thought, looked.

Common filter words found with passive, telling cousins: to see, to hear, could tell, to watch, to decide, to notice, to realize, to wonder, to think, to look.

You don't have to cut every instance of these words, but they are good words to check (and maybe change) if the scene feels told or readers aren't connecting to it.

Step Two: Fix Any Head Hopping or Point of View Shifts

Unless you're writing full third-person omniscient, the rule is one point-of-view character per scene. Check your scenes for any instances where someone other than the point-of-view character has a thought, or expresses (internally) a motive, judgment, or opinion, and thus "shifts" the narrative out of the point-of-view character's head. All the information in that scene should be what the point-of-view character can realistically experience.

This doesn't apply just to third person—first-person writers, watch out for places where the point-of-view character explains another character's motive when it's not logical to have known that motive. If the point-of-view character has no idea a character is going to go to the car "to get his phone" she can't describe his movements that way.

Spotting Point of View Shifts

"To verb" is easy to search for and you'll eliminate a lot of smaller point of view shifts by using "and" instead of "to." For example, "she reached over to pick up the cup" implies motive (how does the narrator *know* she intended to pick up the cup until she did it?). "To verb" often has a non-point-of-view character explaining the motive of another character's action before they physically do it in the scene. Until the character sees it, she can't know why another character is acting.

Other things you can look for:

Any judgment or opinion statements of non-point-of-view characters that aren't in dialogue: A non-point-of-view character will only convey information by what they say and how they act. That's all the point-of-view character can observe.

Places where the point-of-view character states motive or opinion of a non-point-of-view character: If the point-of-view character is guessing or basing her thoughts on what she can observe, then it's probably okay. But if the point-of-view character is attributing a motive as if it's a fact and it's not clear how she'd know, you might be shifting.

The point-of-view character referring to how she looks as if she could see: For example, "my face turned bright pink." Unless she can see it, she can't know what it looks like.

Step Three: Fix Any Inconsistent Points of View

If you use multiple points of view, check for places where your point of view (especially your narrative distance) varies. If you've been in a tight third person for most of the book, but have a few scenes in a distant third, those scenes will jump out at readers and feel out of place (unless there's a good and clear reason for the switch).

Maintain the same point-of-view style throughout the book, and if you need to switch styles or narrative distances, make sure the rules of that switch are clear and consistent.

Step Four: Fix Any Characters Who Know Details They Can't Know

With everything you have to keep track of in a novel, it's understandable that sometimes, you'll accidentally have a character remark on something you forgot to put *into* the novel. Or you'll have characters make huge leaps in logic without having enough groundwork for those leaps to feel credible.

Check your scenes and look for moments (especially big "I figured it out!" moments) to ensure no one has information or is making leaps they couldn't possibly know or make.

Step Five: Fix Any Oddly Self-Aware Character Moments

While some people are good at knowing their motives and analyzing their feelings, most of us aren't that self-aware. We get mad at spouses when we're angry about work, yell at the cat because we did something we're ashamed of, and let past traumas influence our behaviors—we don't realize our bad behavior is due to our fears of abandonment.

Check your scenes for any moments where the character feels too aware of her motives or why she's behaving as she is. Instead, show hints as to the real reason.

Common self-aware red flag words: She knew, she realized, she felt, she thought. Not every instance will be a problem, but it's a good place to start the search.

Step Six: Fix Any Unsubstantiated Emotional Responses

Sometimes a character needs to feel a certain way for the scene, but the groundwork to support that emotion isn't there.

Look for places where your point-of-view character has a strong emotional reaction or feelings about something or someone. If the protagonist can't stand another character, is it clear why? Have there been signs or clues that support why characters feel the way they do? Clarify any responses that feel out of whack.

Step Seven: Fix Any Places Where Characters Are Stating the Obvious

If a character runs into her room, throws herself onto the bed and starts crying, it's a pretty good indication that she's upset. Adding, "She was so upset she thought she'd die" is unnecessary. Since these little phrases tend to slip in when you aren't looking, it's not a bad idea to scan the scenes and look for places where your characters are being a little *too* on the nose.

Step Eight: Fix Any Faulty Character Reactions

This is all about stimulus/response. A character can't respond to something that hasn't happened yet. "Jane dodged out of the way when the zombie lunged at her." Until readers see the zombie lunge, they have no clue why Jane is dodging. Make sure the chronology of the actions unfolds in a logical and clear fashion.

Common stimulus/response red flag words: when, as, before. Revise as needed so the stimulus comes first, *then* the character reaction.

Now that you've caught and fixed any point-of-view and narrator issues, let's get closer and look at any internalization issues.

If You Want to Streamline the Internalization

Internalization is where your characters think and reflect on what's happening to them. It's strong vehicle to show their voices and how their minds work, which helps turn them into real and solid people. Readers get to see the world through the characters' eyes and hear their thoughts about that world.

In this session, the goal is to eliminate any internalization that isn't working, and make sure your characters' thoughts are clear.

Step One: Adjust Any Out-of-Balance Thinking

How much (or how little) thinking a character does in a scene can be a red flag for other issues. It's a good place to start when reviewing your internalization. Be wary if:

The protagonist thinks too much: A thinking-too-much protagonist needs a boot to the butt to get her moving. This type of draft often feels like nothing is happening and readers are waiting for you to get to a point.

Look for scenes where there's a lot of deliberating about what to do. The characters might be talking about the action the protagonist needs to take, and either showing it afterward (making the story repetitious) or skimming through the action itself because it feels like you've already written it. You might even find yourself summarizing the action in a "so we did this" or "after we did this" type fashion.

Take those internal planning sessions and turn them into active scenes. You know what happens, so either skip the planning altogether (often you can) or trim that planning scene down to the bare minimum and let the scene play out in real time.

The protagonist thinks too little: A thinking-too-little protagonist is one who's there to act out plot, but has no feelings about what she's doing. This usually results in a plot that feels aimless, since nothing matters, and there's no sense of stakes to carry the story forward.

Now that you know what happens in your plot, it's time to dig in and let your protagonist say *why* it's important. Look for scenes where:

Choices are made: Choices send the plot in new directions, but without understanding why those choices are made, readers might start wondering why they're following along. Before long, plot events starts to blur and it's hard to remember what's happened since none of it carried enough meaning to sink in. Readers feel lost and ungrounded, and they don't get it.

Make sure your protagonist thinks about what she's doing, weighs the pros and cons, and makes a choice that seems logical to her, *and* keeps readers interested. Provide a sense that the protagonist is acting on her own feelings and needs, driving the story forward toward a personal goal.

Stakes are mentioned: You might say why something is bad, but without context from the protagonist to put it into perspective, readers might not get exactly what "bad" means. Or worse, they might not realize the stakes have escalated at all if the protagonist isn't concerned or does little to say why this is a bad thing. This leads to flat stories that are easy to put down and never pick back up.

Make sure the stakes and how those stakes affect the characters are clear. This is personal for your protagonist, so get into her head and show the how and why. Show the consequences so readers can worry right along with her.

The protagonist is over-thinking everything: Thinking about the past, making witty observations, and chatting with the reader are all ways in which your protagonist might be delaying *doing* something. While it's good to know the reasons behind an action, over-explaining why it matters at every step can indicate you're not sure what action you want the protagonist to take. So you brainstorm on the page by going over it all in her head.

Look for reasons for your protagonist to be thinking those thoughts. Perhaps put her in a scene where getting out of a jam depends on what she's done in the past, allowing you to keep the action moving and still show those deep thoughts. You can also give her a friend (or even an enemy) to talk to and make the conversation part of a larger and more active scene.

Step Two: Check for Judgment and Reactions

Internalization is where the character does her thinking, which usually means she's reacting to something that happened in the story, judging or considering it (or reacting without thinking), and then acting on that information and assumptions made from that information.

While it's unrealistic to go through every line of internalization (unless you're doing a deep edit), there are some red flags you can look for to spot potential problems:

An abundance of pronouns: Excessive pronouns can indicate filtering, especially when combined with filtering red flag words, such as "she felt, I realized, he knew."

An abundance of questions: A litany of internal questions could indicate the character is telling readers what *they* ought to be thinking about instead of showing the character thinking and reacting to it. Often, these questions are unnecessary, and having too many of them will distance readers from the character. A lot of internal questions could also indicate an opportunity to flesh out a character's emotional state so those questions are implied, not stated.

Reasons to Use Internal Questions

When it's something the character would believably ask in that situation: Sometimes people do ask internal questions, especially if angry or upset. "How could he do this to me?" is a good (if clichéd) example. "Is he serious?" is another. Thoughts that could be spoken aloud often work just fine as internal questions, though it's fun to consider how the scene *would* go if the character *did* say them out loud.

When you want to remind readers of the goal: An internal question can work as a scene goal statement: "Where was the murder weapon?" This shows the character is probably going to be looking for this item. "What if she *wasn't* at the bar?" suggests figuring this out is important. It can also tell readers what the overall story question is, and what the plot is trying to resolve: "So what *really* happened to Mario?"

When it would create more mystery, tension, or a dramatic pause: Questions can work as those "dum-dum-DUM!" cliffhanger moments to raise tensions or hook readers. It might be a revelation: "Did that mean John was alive?" Or it could be an internal conflict the character will be struggling with: "Could she trust him?"

When it would show a different attitude or opinion from what the narrator is displaying: Sometimes a character feels one way internally, but is forced (or wants) to show a different attitude or emotion externally. An internal question is one way to show this dichotomy: "You make a good point." She nodded. What kind of moron was he?

When a character is debating with herself: Although you have to be careful here (it's easy to go too far), questions can be a handy way to show a character having an internal debate. This can be especially helpful if you need to show how a character made a connection or a leap in logic that might seem contrived without the explanation.

Reasons *Not* to Use Internal Questions

When they're there solely to lead readers to the conclusion you want them to make: If readers can't get to that question on their own by what they see in the text, and there's no reason (or a weak reason) for the character to ask it, there's a good chance it's going to read awkwardly.

When they're repetitious: Lots of questions in a row can read as if you're badgering readers, especially if they all basically say the same thing. Try showing internal thoughts or actions that suggest those questions (or answers to those questions) instead.

When they don't convey any real information to move the story: Empty internal questions can feel like empty dialogue. They're not necessary to understand anything in the scene, but they feel like they ought to be said. Try cutting them and seeing which versions read better.

When they're redundant: If the internal question is followed up by thoughts, action, or dialogue that implies the same question, there's no need to shine a light on it. For example, if the character is staring at a crime scene and describing it in detail, starting or ending with, "What happened here?" isn't necessary.

If you're not sure if the question should stay or go, ask:

- Does the scene read well without the question?
- Is it shoving the idea/thought/mystery in the reader's face?
- Would the reader ask the same question from seeing what's in the scene?
- Does it feel awkward?

If you answered yes to any of these, odds are you can cut it.

Internal questions show what a character is struggling with and what she's trying to do, but they can be overused if you aren't careful. Trust your instincts—if it feels awkward or melodramatic, it probably is and cutting it would strengthen the scene (reading it out loud is a good test for melodrama).

Step Three: Examine Italicized Text

Immediate thoughts are often italicized, so a search for italicized text could help spot any internal dialogue that isn't working, or which could be stronger as internalization. Often, a simple tense change can turn internal dialogue into internalization, such as *Is he asking me out?* vs. Was he asking her out?

⚑ **REVISION RED FLAG:** Italicized thoughts should be used sparingly (some advise not doing it at all, but this is a personal taste issue). If you find a high percentage of italicized thoughts, or most of the internalization is in italics, there's a problem or a misuse of internal dialogue. Look for ways to shift those thoughts into the narrative and eliminate all but the most critical italicized thoughts.

Revision Option: Internalization and Voice

How characters think and what they notice, from their internal thoughts to the narrative itself, is where voice thrives. The always-distracted scatterbrain is going to see the world differently from the detail-oriented observer, and their voices will reflect that.

You'll cover voice in more depth in Workshop Four: Dialogue and Voice, but here are some things to keep in mind as you revise your internalization:

What does the point-of-view character typically think about? This can show how her thought process works, what she worries about, or what distracts her.

What types of words best fit or exemplify the point-of-view character's personality? A sports fanatic might use a lot of sports terms or metaphors, or a quiet, shy type might have a cutting wit hiding behind the shyness. Look for language that shows who that character is.

What type of sentence structure best fits the point-of-view character? The person who thinks in short, choppy sentences is different from the one who waxes poetically about her emotions.

What does the character's dialogue sound like? This is a good way to show someone whose inner self differs from the person she shows the world.

Some elements of who you are as a writer will naturally seep in (which is good, as your own voice is important), but each of your characters will have different personalities and see the world in different ways. Just like you use the right verb and the right noun to craft a well-written sentence, use the right words and phrasing to craft a well-developed character voice.

You've been working on characters for a while now, so let's shift gears and focus more on how those characters sound.

Workshop Four: Dialogue and Voice Work

The Goal of This Workshop: To examine the manuscript's dialogue and character voices, and craft believable conversations and unique voices.

What We'll Discuss in This Workshop: Common dialogue pitfalls and ways to correct them, and ways to develop strong voices for your characters.

Welcome to Workshop Four: Dialogue and Voice Work

Dialogue is connected to nearly every aspect of a novel—from how characters convey information, to how they interact, to how they move the plot from scene to scene. When it works, you have real people guiding your readers through the story. When it doesn't, you have bad actors on a cheap stage.

How a character sounds helps readers identify who that character is—in a literal and philosophical sense. Characters who sound the same are hard to tell apart, and can leave readers confused about who is saying what. Bland characters can also rob the story of its uniqueness, offering nothing but cookie cutter people who do nothing to affect the world they live in. They're there to spout their lines, though it doesn't matter which one says what, since they all sound exactly alike and say whatever is required to check off elements on a plot list.

Strong, well-developed characters deserve strong, well-developed voices. Take advantage of all the work you put into them and make sure they sound as real as they feel.

Analyze the Dialogue

Stilted dialogue can stop a story cold or make it sound melodramatic and cheesy. Good dialogue captures the essence of real-life conversations without the awkward pauses and interruptions that actually happen.

In this session, the goal is to examine your dialogue and identify weak spots.

You'll look at the external dialogue, as well as character voices.

Determine if the Dialogue is Working

Dialogue walks a fine line between sounding realistic and conveying necessary information. It's easy to slip over that line into infodumping and character lectures, or have characters who sound like they're reading from a script.

Look over the dialogue in each scene and ask:

- **Do the characters sound like real people?** Real people speak from their own world experience and personal views; they don't read lines on a page. Look for dialogue that sounds forced, overly formal, or stilted. A lack of contractions often indicates too-formal dialogue, as does always speaking in grammatically perfect sentences.
- **Is the dialogue an *actual* conversation or two people stating information at one another for the reader's benefit?** Conversations have give and take, with one character speaking and another responding to what was said. Look for stretches of one long speech followed by another long speech in reply. Characters should be talking, not spouting information.
- **Are characters telling each other what they already know?** Look for any infodumps through dialogue and "as you know, Bob" conversations, and either cut or rework so it sounds natural.

▶ **Are there empty dialogue phrases?** Look for pointless small talk, unnecessary greetings and farewells, and awkward prompts to speak. Trim out the dialogue that does nothing to serve the story.

▶ **Is the dialogue advancing the plot or story?** A conversation might be interesting, but if it isn't serving the story, it's bogging the pacing down. Make sure your characters' conversations have a point to them.

▶ **Are the dialogue tags clear?** Look for spots where the speaker is ambiguous or it's hard to know who's speaking.

▶ **Are there too many dialogue tags?** Only tag where necessary. Also look for places where characters repeatedly use names. If it's clear who's speaking without the tag, cut it.

▶ **Are there any over-written or impossible dialogue tags?** Tags should be simple and words you can physically "say." For example, yelled is a manner of speech, sigh is not. You can't sigh a line of dialogue, but you can yell it. Look for any places where you're trying too hard not to use some form of "she said."

▶ **Are characters giving away too much information for no reason?** Be wary of characters who answer questions with as much information as they can. Not only is it unrealistic, but it could also indicate infodumps through dialogue or places where the goal is achieved too easily.

▶ **Are you summarizing any conversations instead of dramatizing them?** Watch out for conversations explained instead of dramatized. Dialogue is active and keeps the story moving. Summarizing when the characters are standing right there seems told and static.

▶ **Is there subtext? Is it clear what's *not* being said?** Good dialogue is more than what's said, it's also what's not said. Look for places where too much is revealed and nothing is being held back.

▶ **Is the language appropriate for the intended market?** A middle grade novel with a lot of swearing and sexual innuendo is going to have problems with its intended audience. Make sure the language fits who'll be reading it.

Problems Found?

If you find any dialogue issues, spend some time doing the exercises in If You Want to Strengthen the Dialogue on page 114.

Analyze the Voice

Voice is important in a novel, but there's more than your author's voice. Characters have voices too, and making those voices distinct helps readers keep track of who's who. It's also a good way to help you develop your characters into solid personalities. Knowing what they sound like can help determine who they are (and vice versa).

In this session, the goal is to identify weak or too-similar voices in your manuscript.

Determine if the Characters' Voices Are Working

A character's personality is at the core of his or her voice, so keep in mind who a character is as you develop your voices. Look at your characters and ask:

- **Does each point-of-view character have his or her own voice and style of speaking?** Be wary of characters who all sound the same, especially in multiple point-of-view novels. Look for ways to vary how characters speak and interact with other characters.
- **Can you tell who's speaking even without identifying the character by name?** The goal is for readers to know who a character is, even without a name. It's the individual speaking style, verbal ticks, the tangible elements that make one person sound different from another.
- **Can you get a sense of who the character is by the voice?** Personality shines through in how we speak, even if we use the same exact words. Make sure the characters sound like the type of person they are (or are trying to be).
- **Does the point-of-view character's outer voice sound like her internal one?** Unless the character is trying to appear as a different person, the internal and external voices will be similar. Variations due to social situations and direct attempts to hide a true personality

are acceptable, but watch out for interior voices that sound nothing at all like the way a character speaks.

▶ **Do characters use language suitable to their status, age, or cultural situation?** Characters should speak in ways appropriate to their life experiences and place in the world. For example, five-year-old children don't typically sound like college professors unless there's a reason.

▶ **Does the voice change depending on the situation?** A teen sounds different when talking with peers versus talking to parents or authority figures. Are there situations where a character's voice will change? Are there rules for that in your story or world?

▶ **Do the non-point-of-view characters all sound the same?** If you can change the speaker and it doesn't change how the dialogue is spoken, the character voices probably aren't varied enough. While some lines might be interchangeable, most shouldn't be. Aim for every character expressing themselves in a distinctive way.

▶ **Are any of the character voices annoying?** Be wary of whiney, mean, overly sarcastic, or otherwise attitude-laden characters. A little goes a long way, and it's easy to push a strong personality into an irritating character (young adult and women's fiction authors be especially wary of this).

▶ **Are any of the character voices stereotyped or clichéd?** Does the jock sound like a bully? The cop tough and hardnosed? The librarian meek and mousy? People speak in ways that show who they are (or who they want people to think they are). Avoid the voices we've all seen before.

▶ **Is there an overabundance of dialect?** Dialect is hard to read and often unnecessary. A word here and there to establish an accent can work, but if readers need a translator to understand the character, it's gone too far.

▶ **Does every character use the same vocabulary or is it varied?** Different cultures and educational backgrounds will influence what words a person uses. Your poor farmer from the lowlands shouldn't use the same words and phrases as the royal princess with the private tutor.

▶ **Does every character speak with the same rhythm or pattern?** Someone born and raised in Manhattan sounds different from someone raised in Mississippi. Does a character use clipped sentences or does she ramble? Is she curt? Eloquent?

 **REVISION RED FLAG:** Pay attention to the voices of secondary and non-point-of-view characters. Often, they have little variance in voice.

Problems Found?

If you find any voice issues, spend some time doing the exercises in If You Want to Vary the Voices on page 120.

If You Want to Strengthen the Dialogue

Dialogue makes up a sizable chunk of a novel, but it's also a common area to find weak prose. In first drafts, it's not unusual to let your characters ramble on, give them unrealistic dialogue, and even steal their unique voices from them.

In this session, the goal is to clean up and strengthen your dialogue.

Step One: Eliminate Empty Dialogue

In real life conversations, people use small talk and break up what they say into bites. For example:

> "Hi."
>
> "Hey, John."
>
> "Did you see that new movie?"
>
> "The one with the robot?"
>
> "Yeah."
>
> "Not yet, you?"

In a novel, this will slow the pace down and make readers impatient to get back to the story (and use a lot of unnecessary words). Realistic dialogue is condensed to keep the pace moving:

> "Hey, John. Did you see the new movie with the robot?"
>
> "Not yet, you?"

This takes a lot fewer words to get to the same place, and nothing in the story is lost.

Look through your dialogue for any lines that can be condensed, combined, or cut. The beginning of a conversation is a common place to find empty dialogue, as characters get up to speed to have the real talk. Also check the ends of conversations as they wrap it up and say goodbye.

If you're unsure if the dialogue is needed or not, ask:

If you took it out, would the meaning of the conversation change? Empty dialogue is empty because it adds nothing to what's being said.

Could you combine several lines into one, tighter line that accomplishes the same task? If four lines basically say, "Hello, how are you, long time no see," or the like, then one line is probably all you need. Skip the delays and get to the meat of the conversation.

Are you *trying* to delay the scene? Sometimes you add empty dialogue because you want the scene to convey someone dragging her feet. Instead of throwing in words that mean nothing, look for ways to deepen the scene or add additional information *while* giving the impression of time passing awkwardly.

One benefit to empty dialogue is that it's easy to get rid of since it's not necessary. If you're trying to trim down your word count, this is a good thing to add to your words-to-cut list.

Step Two: Revise Stilted or Too-Formal Dialogue

Overly formal dialogue often appears when you're trying to sound "writerly" and forget that characters should sound like real people.

Go through any dialogue that doesn't sound like real people talking and rework to sound natural. Use contractions and sentence fragments, let characters interrupt each other, and make sure the conversations sound like conversations.

Step Three: Revise "Share Everything" Conversations

Not every character should be forthcoming about every bit of information she knows. Real people lie, they fudge, they withhold information, they steer conversations back to what *they're* interested in (usually themselves), and they don't offer information that will make them look bad.

Review character conversations and revise anything that's a little too helpful or forthcoming. Consider what a character might be hiding or trying to achieve in the scene or conversation. Not only will you make the conversations more interesting, but you'll likely raise the tension and conflict as well.

Things to consider:

What's more interesting if it's left unsaid? Look for opportunities to add in subtext that deepens the scene.

How does the body language underscore or contradict what's being said? Our bodies can give us away when we're lying, or support us when we're telling the truth. Someone who sounds cheerful and agreeable while clenching her jaw and hands is sending mixed signals.

Where might characters lie or hide information? Even if they're not trying to hurt the protagonist, characters can cause trouble by wanting to keep secrets.

What are characters afraid to say? Dancing around an issue can heighten tension and create conflict in a scene. It also helps develop character.

Step Four: Revise Awkward Summarized Dialogue

Dialogue is about the spoken word, but once in a while you might gloss over it and summarize a conversation when you don't need to. It's another form of telling, and often readers want to see these conversations unfold in real time in the novel. For example, I walked into the kitchen and asked Mom about the gun I'd found in her suitcase. She dodged the question and asked me what I wanted on my eggs instead.

This is a missed opportunity to create tension and probably a compelling moment in the novel. What would Mom say? How would she dodge the question? What was her body language like?

Look for any summarized dialogue and dramatize sections that would be stronger if seen.

Step Five: Eliminate Infodumps as Dialogue

Infodumping doesn't just happen to prose. Look for characters talking about subjects they'd never talk about. A good rule of thumb: If the information is for the *reader's* benefit, chances are you're dumping. If the information is for the character's benefit (or detriment), chances are it's fine. For example:

Reader's benefit: "I'll rig up a small explosive device to blow open the door. That's the way we did it when I was deployed in Afghanistan as a Navy SEAL."

Character's benefit: "Um, Kevin, where'd you learn to make bombs?"

"The Navy."

One advantage to *not* explaining everything to readers is that they won't know exactly what's going on or what's going to happen. If they don't know, then they'll read in anticipation of what will happen next. Don't explain the magic trick before you perform it.

Common places to find infodumps in dialogue:

"As you know, Bob" conversations: Look for characters explaining in detail what both characters already know. Find ways to convey the information naturally, while at the same time, giving readers the important details.

Catch-up dialogue: One character finds out critical information the other characters need to know, but *not* having them tell the others would seem odd, and readers might wonder how the other person learned about it. Try adding more information or giving the reader something new so it isn't so repetitive. Or use slightly different language so you're not repeating what you just showed in another scene.

If you have to dump information into your dialogue, keep it in the character's voice.

Step Six: Revise Awkward or Confusing Dialogue Tags

Dialogue tags are part of any novel, keeping them from sounding repetitive can be a challenge. Said gets old fast. Nodded, shrugged, frowned, and smiled can only be used so often. Having a character push back her hair or clench his hands clogs up the narrative after a bit and can even seem melodramatic. Too much stage direction feels clunky, but not enough makes a scene unclear.

Dialogue tags work best when they're invisible—either by not drawing attention to themselves or by blending in and doing more than identifying the speaker. The harder *they* work, the less work *you* have to do to craft the scene.

Bad dialogue tags can range from cumbersome to ridiculous, creating missed opportunities to flesh out a scene.

Common areas to check for trouble:

He said adverbidly: In most cases, an adverb in a dialogue tag is a missed opportunity to show, not tell. Check your tags and make sure you have good reasons for any adverbs used, and there isn't a better way to dramatize the adverb instead.

Non-said tags: Said is a perfectly good word. It's invisible to readers, so they gloss right over it. Avoiding it, or using solely action dialogue tags, can give the prose a clunky, list-like feel since it's technically one short sentence after another.

Internalization overload: Internalization tags dialogue without using said or stage direction, but be wary of large chunks of internal thought that create awkwardly long pauses between bits of dialogue. If there are nine lines of thought between "Did you go?" and "Yes, I did," readers might forget what the character was asking about.

Characters as mind readers: Sometimes a character will think something, but the other characters in the scene react as if the words were spoken. Make sure characters act based on dialogue they heard.

Awkward dialogue tag placement: Tagging every line of dialogue at the end feels repetitious and list-like. Listen to how the words flow and look for the right spot to add a pause, since a tag often works like a comma to slow the dialogue down. Ask yourself if you can you get more dramatic punch if the tag is in a different place. This is especially true for zingers or those "dum-dum-DUM!" moments.

The goal with dialogue and tags is to find a balance between them. Use enough exposition to set the scene and make it clear who's talking, but not so much that it detracts from what's being said. Let the stage direction add to the suspense of the scene and provide details that flesh out the setting instead of just sitting there.

A general rule of thumb (and this can vary by genre and story): Anything more than six exchanges of dialogue in a row without a break risks losing readers. The longer the conversation, the faster it will likely overwhelm them. Be particularly wary of long passages with characters speaking *at* each other instead of having a conversation (as in dumping information or backstory via dialogue).

Step Seven: Flesh Out Talking Head Conversations

Sometimes a conversation reads like two heads talking with no sense of place. Look for passages with a lot of dialogue but no description or additional information. Add enough dialogue tags, description, and stage direction to ground readers in the scene. If you find a lot of these scenes, consider doing the exercises in *Book Three: Fixing Your Setting and Description Problem*.

Step Eight: Prune Unnecessary Dialogue

Dialogue is a critical part of a story, so it's rare to have too much. What's more likely is either dialogue that isn't helping convey the story, or there's too *little* of something else—too little internalization, description, stage direction, or action. If you think there's too much dialogue, check to see what might have gotten left out.

Also check for "too much dialogue" sections filled with empty dialogue. You'll often find a lot of small talk that can easily be trimmed out.

REVISION TIP: *Zoom out on your page and see if you have a lot of short lines or a nice mix of lines and gray areas (where a text paragraph looks like a gray box). A dialogue-heavy/narrative-sparse page will have a lot of white space and look more like a list than a page from a novel.*

Many dialogue issues can be found by reading the scene out loud. Awkward phrases tangle our tongues, alliteration hits our ears funny, and telling speakers apart becomes much harder. Also, if you get a little winded or forget who's speaking, that's a red flag that there isn't enough text to support all that dialogue.

Once your dialogue is looking and sounding good, move on to your character voices.

If You Want to Vary the Voices

Fantastic character voices can overcome minor flaws in a novel, because readers will forgive the sins of a story for characters they love to hang out with. That doesn't mean you can slack off on writing a strong book, but it does take some of the pressure off getting it perfect.

In this session, the goal is to develop strong voices for all the characters who need them.

Step One: Vary Too-Similar Character Voices

Ideally, characters should sound as different as they look, but it's not uncommon to have secondary characters with basically the same voice. You could change who says a line of dialogue and not have to change the dialogue itself. For example, "Maybe this is a bad idea," Bland Character said.

If you had to describe the way a character spoke, how would you do it? Describe the type of character and what he or she sounds like. Your gut reaction can guide you in determining the right voice for each character.

Revision Option: Ways to Develop Character Voices

Character voices bring our character to life, so it's important that they sound like the unique people they are.

Start with the character's general personality: The voice will reflect that personality and color every line of dialogue and internal thought. Even better, it'll help you develop richer characters because they won't be two-dimensional people spouting lines on a page. Those lines will come from someplace real, because you'll know why those characters speak like they do.

Consider how the character greets people: People say hello differently. Sometimes it's a regional or cultural tradition, or even a personal style. Is your character a "Yo what's up?" kind of gal, or a, "So good to see you," type? How she greets someone suggests where she grew up, where she lives now, and how open she is toward others.

If she's a boisterous greeter, she's boisterous in other ways as well. Or maybe she likes to draw attention to herself, so she's the one who interrupts or always has something to add to a conversation. If she gives a weak, "Hi," then she might be the quiet one who rarely gives more than a one- or two-word answer.

Consider how the character answers questions: Does she give one-word answers or way-too-much information? Does she get right to the point or is there a story attached to it? Someone who's reluctant to answer might also be a gal who doesn't like to talk a lot or reveal too much about herself. A gal who says *too* much might be a talker in all aspects of her life and have a hard time getting to a point. The reluctant gal might be a "Hey" kind of greeter, while the Chatty Cathy probably never *just* says hello.

Consider how the character reacts to situations: Someone who faces a situation and immediately decides what to do is a different personality type from someone who questions it before making a decision. The jump-to-it gal always "knows" what to do (even when she's wrong) and might sound bossy or confident. The thoughtful gal might appear hesitant or meek (even when she's not) or might seem wise because she always asks the right questions.

Consider the character's education level: Education plays a role in how people communicate. Is this a gal with a large vocabulary who likes to use it, or someone with a limited vocabulary who uses a lot of slang or clichés? Take it a step further and think about why she speaks as she does. Maybe she's self-conscious about her Ph.D. and purposefully tries to sound dumber to fit in. Or she might be a smart gal who never graduated high school who tries hard to sound more educated.

Maybe that boisterous greeter who makes statements instead of asking questions is insecure about her lack of education, and overcompensates by always acting like she knows what to do or what's going on. Or the meek greeter asks questions because she's not sure she understands what's happening and doesn't want to appear dumb. The friendly greeter might ask a lot of questions to determine the best course of action, because she truly wants to help and has the smarts to offer good advice. (See how these all build upon each other?)

Consider where the character grew up: Where a character grew up will leave traces on her speech. If her hometown has a distinct accent or speaking pattern, it makes it even easier to determine how someone from there would speak. Saying pop versus soda, crayfish versus crawdad, everyone versus y'all.

Consider how the character organizes thoughts and words: A thoughtful thinker might be precise in how she speaks, while a free spirit might ramble or use vague, poetic terms. Careless personalities probably speak without thinking, while control freaks want to make sure everyone understands exactly what they're saying.

Consider the character's favorite sayings or quips: People use different expressions and react in different ways. Maybe one character swears, and another is genteel. One might relate every situation to stories her grandmother once told, or pepper her speech with another language. Look for common expressions and revise so each character has a unique way of expressing themselves (within reason, of course. Some expressions are universal).

Step Two: Develop the Voices of Non-Point-of-View Characters

Voice is a bit harder for non-point-of-view characters because internalization is a large part of character voice, and without that, you have to rely on the dialogue and how your point-of-view character sees and hears that character. But there *are* ways to help differentiate your characters and know what dialogue and traits go with what person.

Revision Option: Ways to Develop Voices in Non-Point-of-View Characters

You'll see voice exhibited through dialogue and body language in non-point-of-view characters. Look for ways to:

Reflect the type of information the character typically conveys: If she often has the answers to technical questions, her voice is going to reflect those technical skills. If she's more the trust-your-emotions kind of confidant, her voice will reflect that trust-your-gut attitude.

Support the character's role in the story: A character's role and relationship to the protagonist influences the voice. The best friend will interact with the protagonist differently than the antagonist or the love interest would. A comic relief character will be funny, while a cautionary tale mirror character might echo the darker traits of the protagonist.

Limit (or increase) how much you want that character to stand out: Strong voices draw attention, so be wary if a small, walk-on character is more memorable than a major character. The most important characters should have the strongest and clearest voices. Make sure you have the right balance of attention.

Character personality shines through no matter what that character is doing or saying, so take advantage of all the opportunities you have to show who your characters are.

Now that you've revised your characters and the elements associated with them, let's look at your overall word count.

Workshop Five: Word Count Work

The Goal of This Workshop: To determine if you need to adjust the word count of your manuscript.

What We'll Discuss in This Workshop: How to cut words from a too-long manuscript, and how to add words and flesh out a too-short manuscript.

Welcome to Workshop Five: Word Count Work

Word counts provide a framework for your novel and a guide to your chosen genre, but the goal is to tell your story to the best of your ability, however many words that is. If a word isn't pulling its weight, cut it. If it's a star performer, let it shine.

Your novel should grab readers from the start, offer them a story they can't put down, and hold that attention until the end. The trick is to make sure every word you use does exactly that. If you have 75,000 words that don't grab a reader, the book will fail, but if you have 140,000 words that grab a reader and don't let go, the book will succeed. It's the story that matters. A great book is a great book.

That said, a published novel *is* a product, and as a product, certain rules apply. These rules exist, for example, to cover the cost of making the book versus what it can sell for, and a book that will cost twice as much due to size isn't economical to sell. Readers won't pay thirty dollars for a 2,500-page paperback (never mind how they'd even *hold* the thing). With e-books and e-book-only publishers, word counts are changing, but the guidelines still do exist, and if you plan to pursue a traditional publishing path, you do need to consider all facets of that.

No matter which path you take, ultimately, it's not how many words you have, but what those words do, that counts.

Analyze the Size of the Novel

When determining the right size for a novel, consider the general ranges of your chosen genre. They will guide you to what readers—and publishers—expect. You want every word used to help the story. It's not about reaching a certain limit, it's about writing the best story you can.

In this session, the goal is to see if your word count is within your target market range and personal goal, and adjust if need be.

A word about word counts: Some writers will be revising a novel with a particular genre, market, or publishing path in mind and need to be within a certain range to sell or publish it. For example, category romances have specific rules that must be adhered to for a particular imprint. If you're not one of those writers, you're not as constrained by word count.

Determine if Your Word Count is Working

Word counts for a typical novel run between 80,000 and 100,000 words. If your novel falls in that range, chances are you're fine for most adult fiction genres and markets. Children's fiction runs 30,000 to 50,000 for middle grade, and 50,000 to 80,000 for young adult. Chapter books run 5,000 to 25,000 words. Picture books come in at under 500. Mysteries often go as low as 60,000 and historical fiction and epic fantasy rise as high as 140,000.

These are *very* general ranges, but if the average size of the genre and market you're aiming for is 60,000 words, your 120,000-word novel is too long. That's like trying to pitch a movie for a 60-second commercial slot.

Be wary of the word-count trap. For every person who says, "You'll never get published with a 145,000-word novel," another will say, "But BestsellerBob's book was 145,000 words." It does happen, but it's important to remember that those novels succeeded *in spite of the word count,* not because of it. You stand a much better chance at success if you fall within the norms, but if the novel absolutely without a doubt must be that size, then, let it be that size. Just understand that it could be an issue down the road if you plan to publish.

Your chosen publishing path—traditional or self—also affects what's an acceptable word count for your novel. For example, if your goal is a traditional publisher, staying within the standard ranges gives you the best chance at selling your novel. If you plan to submit to an e-book-only publisher or self-publish, word counts can fall outside the norm. No paper means no printing costs and no bulky books, so additional pages aren't as problematic.

Problems Found?

If you find you want to cut back on your word count, spend some time doing the exercises in If You Want to Cut Words From the Manuscript on page 127. If you find you want to increase your word count, spend some time doing the exercises in If You Want to Add Words to the Manuscript on page 131.

If You Want to Cut Words From the Manuscript

Cutting words from your manuscript doesn't have to be a huge hack and slash deal. You don't have to rip your baby to shreds. In fact, hacking away whole scenes often hurts more than helps, because you're killing the story, not the extra words. You want to get rid of the words that *aren't* helping the story.

In this session, the goal is to trim down your manuscript to your target word count range without losing any of your story.

Cutting Words Isn't so Hard. No, Really.

Cutting thousands of words from your manuscript seems daunting, and cutting *tens of thousands* of words can make you want to curl up in a ball and cry, but it's much easier than you think.

Let's look at what "cutting words" really means:

A common "too-long" manuscript is 120,000-words, roughly 480 pages (based on the traditional 250 words-per-page format). You can cut 4,800 words if you delete ten words per page. Ten words is nothing—it's one sentence in most cases, and even in polished and published novels you can still find one sentence per page that can go and not lose any important information. Cut twenty words per page and that's almost 10,000 words gone with little effort. A 150,000-word novel? 600 pages, and 6,000 or 12,000 words gone. Cut thirty words—18,000 words down.

Approaching your edit on a words-per-page basis is much more manageable and allows you to trim consistently across the entire novel, not just certain sections of it.

Step One: Decide How Much You Want to Cut

You might have a fixed number in mind, such as 90,000 words, or a range, such as 80,000-90,000 words. You might also decide to cut in stages, taking out half of the target and then seeing how the manuscript flows before doing anything else.

Step Two: Decide Where it Needs Cutting

Most manuscripts can be trimmed overall, but some will be heavy in one area and need specific trimming. Looking at the novel's structure is an easy way to determine where the extra words are coming from.

Using the basic Three-Act Structure, list the word count of each act (or use whatever structure you prefer and adjust your percentages to fit your structure). Act One is the first 25 percent of the manuscript. The second 25 percent fills the ramp up in act two to the midpoint. The third 25 percent is the ramp down in Act Two from the midpoint. The final 25 percent is in Act Three. So, if your manuscript is 100,000 words, you'd have four chunks of 25,000 words each. At the end of each act, you'd have a major plot turning point.

Remember—these guidelines aren't exact, but if (using the above example) you discover the first act is 35,000 words, but the rest fits the target size for your novel, there's a good chance the beginning is too long and your extra words should be cut from there.

A 10 percent variance in size is fairly normal, but anything beyond that bears a closer look. If you decide an act is working even though it's longer, that's okay. The goal is to use structure to diagnose and identify potential trouble areas, not force your manuscript to fit a particular template.

Step Three: Cut Down the Manuscript

Now comes the tough part, but you can do it. Take it step by step, page by page, and be ruthless. If your instincts tell you what needs to go first, trust them.

Common Areas for Extra Words

Extra words can be found anywhere, but there are a few places where writers tend to babble. Check these areas first when trimming words.

Stage direction in dialogue tags: If the speaker is clear, getting rid of the "she said" tag can help eliminate hundreds of words.

Repeated ideas or thoughts: It's not uncommon to say the same thing in different ways in a scene. Look for multiple details in descriptions, emotional internalizations, and introductions of pretty much anything—these are frequently areas to pile on extra information.

Unnecessary or redundant words: For example, is someone sitting down on the floor? If so, down can go—unless something weird is going on with gravity, sitting on the floor *always* means down. Check your prepositions as well, as most of those can go.

Extra description: A few implied words are often enough to give readers the idea of what something looks like. Let them fill in the blanks so you can save the words.

Characters questioning themselves: Often narrators and protagonists will ask what they should do or wonder about something. It usually reads a lot like them talking to themselves. More times than not, you can trim out these phrases or combine them so they use fewer words.

Overwriting: Look for places where one word can replace several, such as "we went around back to the rear of the store" vs. "We went behind the store."

Tightening the overall writing eliminates the extra words without changing anything.

Revision Option: Tricks to Make Cutting Words Easier

If your words-to-cut number is daunting, it might help to trick your brain into thinking it's not as bad as it looks.

Do the easy cuts first: Empty words, empty dialogue, unnecessary tags—cut all the words that commonly bloat a novel first. You might be surprised at how many "only" "just" and "of the" a novel has.

Cut back to front: If you're cutting words-per-page, start on the last page and work your way toward the beginning. Not only will this keep you from getting caught up in the story, it also won't adjust the page and cause you to cut more words from the front than the back as the novel tightens and becomes shorter.

Cut one chapter at a time in a new file: Copy the chapter into a new file before you trim. It's a lot easier to hit that goal when you can see those words dripping off. And a bonus: By isolating the chapter, you can look at it more objectively and judge the pacing and flow.

Cut one act at a time in a new file: Same principle, with more pages. This can help ensure the cuts are applied evenly throughout the novel.

Set time limits on your cutting sessions: The longer you edit, the more likely it is you'll let something slide because you're tired and want to move on to the next part. Take a break between editing sessions and avoid this temptation.

It's not unusual to need several editing passes to cut down a manuscript. The easiest words tend to go first. Then, if you still need to trim, you have to make harder and harder decisions.

If you need to add words, move on to the next session.

If You Want to Add Words to the Manuscript

We spend a lot of time talking about what to cut from our manuscripts, but there are times when we do need to add words. Maybe you have a novella you want to make larger, or a NaNo (National Novel Writing Month) novel that needs fleshing out, or you fell short of your genre's target range. Even if a novel is the right size for the intended market and genre, you might think the story needs deepening to make it stronger.

In this session, the goal is to find the best way to add words to your manuscript without hurting the story or bloating the narrative.

Step One: Diagnose What's Missing

Before you add anything, determine if you have a sparse manuscript that needs some fleshing out, or a novel that's short on plot. A sparse novel may not need any macro work, while a short-on-plot novel will need some larger additions. Your editorial map will help here, as will your draft analysis from Workshop One.

Plot Check: Look at your plot. Is it too easy to go from inciting event to resolution? Did you skip any steps? If you haven't, do any events need a step or two more to accomplish?

Look for places where if the protagonist didn't win, or outcomes didn't go in her favor, you could tack on a scene or two and add more conflict. Be cautious here though, because you don't want scenes that *take* longer, there needs to be real conflict.

Also look for places where the stakes will go up if the protagonist fails instead of succeeds. Or places where you can raise the stakes if she fails. You want to maintain that sense of problems getting worse and worse or you'll end up with a lot of empty "stuff" happening that doesn't move the story forward.

Subplot Check: Take a peek at your subplots. Are there any points on your main plot line that can be complicated or hindered by braiding in an existing subplot? Can you deepen any of them to give something else in the novel greater meaning? Can they affect the stakes? Do you *have* any subplots? The amount of subplots varies by genre and book, but on average, you usually see one or two subplots in a novel.

Tangent Check: Were there any scenes with goals or ideas you started to explore but decided against it? Those might be subplot ideas your subconscious thought would be fun to develop but didn't, which could be exactly the subplot you need.

Conflict Check: Look for spots where decisions are made. Are the choices too easy? How can you make them harder? And not just physically harder, but emotionally tougher as well.

Clarity Check: Is everything clear? Is the stage direction solid and can readers follow what's happening in every scene? Are the dialogue tags clear so there's no confusion over who's speaking? Is there enough backstory to inform readers about the significance of events? Often these elements get left out because you're terrified of having too much.

World Building Check: This is true for real worlds as well as crafted worlds. Have you done enough with your setting so the world feels real? Real-world writers—have you used enough specific details to make your setting come alive? It's easy to say "New York" and let readers fill in the blanks, but you could end up with flat and lifeless worlds that way. And if your world is created, then you might find some confused readers who feel ungrounded, especially if you used a lot of made-up words.

Internalization Check: Are you in your point-of-view character's head enough? You know why your characters act as they do, but are you getting that all on the page? Pretend you know nothing about them or their history. Are the details readers need to know clear? Short novels often have lots of action, but the emotional aspect is missing—and vice versa.

Action Check: Are you in your point-of-view character's head *too* much? Are you telling or summarizing what's happening and not letting it unfold? Strange as it sounds, action scenes can be boring to write, so it's easy to scrimp on them to get to the more interesting emotional scenes.

But it's the balance between head and heart that make the story work.

Backstory Check: Is there an element of the backstory that might be dramatized or illustrated to shed new or better light on something already in the novel? You don't need to add a flashback (unless you do), but a memory of something might cause a different action or response somewhere and take the story to a new place, or even offer a new obstacle to overcome.

Step Two: Flesh Out Where Needed

Once you've identified what's missing, return to the specific workshops and redo the exercises until your manuscript is the right size for the story you want to tell.

The key thing to remember when you're bulking up a novel is to be true to the story. Look for ways to tell that story, deepen those characters, and keep readers guessing what will happen next.

All that's left now is to take one, final look at your manuscript.

Workshop Six:
A Final Look

The Goal of This Workshop: To do a final review to catch any issues not previously caught and fixed.

What We'll Discuss in This Workshop: How to know if you're done revising, and how to review your manuscript like a reader.

Welcome to Workshop Six: A Final Look

By the time you get to the final look, you probably want it over. You're sick of the novel, you're tired, and you want to move on to the next step (this is normal, so don't worry). It's a dangerous time, because the urge to send the manuscript out—either to agents, editors, or publishing it ourselves—is high.

Resist the urge.

This is when those "I can't believe I didn't catch that" mistakes happen. You stop seeing what's on the page and see what you want or expect to see. You ignore any nagging thoughts that you *should* fix that subplot, or third chapter ending, or too-similar names, and tell yourself no one will notice.

And someone always does.

Take a break from revising if you need to (a good idea, as it lets you forget what you wanted to do and see what's there), then come back and look at that finished draft and decide if it truly is finished.

Are the Revisions Done?

How do you *know* when a novel is done? When *do* you stop revising? Ultimately that's up to the writer, but you usually have a sense of when you're making novel-changing edits and when you're delaying the inevitable. Declaring a novel "finished" carries a lot of weight and even expectations, so it can be as scary as it is exhilarating. Sometimes, you'd rather keep fiddling with it than send it out.

In this session, the goal is to determine if you are indeed finished with your revision. If you know you're done, skip this session and move onto the final read through.

The easiest way to tell if you're done is to look at the type of changes you're still making.

If You're Making Minor Changes

If all you're doing is tweaking a word here and a comma there—style changes not substance—you're probably done. However, one or two tweaks per page suggests one last proof-reading pass will benefit you. One or two tweaks per chapter suggests it's probably good to go. One caveat here: If the tweaks are errors, keep proofing until you get them all.

If You're Making Story Changes

If you're still tweaking the story, the revisions are not done. In fact, if the story is changing significantly at this stage, that's a red flag that the novel itself isn't finished. You might need to nail down the story and fix it before you can return to the revision.

If You're Making Text Changes

If you're still getting the text right, revising sentences, or moving text around, the revisions *could* be done. If the tweaking isn't changing the story or scenes any, you can skip ahead and polish the text—approach it as a proofreader or copy editor. If the tweaks change the meaning of the sentences and scenes, then you're still revising.

If You're Making Word Count Changes

If you still need to adjust the word count (up or down), the revisions are not done.

If You're Making "Scared it's Not Good Enough" Changes

If you're tweaking out of fear, you're probably done revising. This is a normal fear, and self-doubt about a new project happens to pretty much everyone.

If You're Making "It's Not Quite Right" Changes

If everything *feels* like it's done, but there's something that still bugs you, it could go either way.

On one hand, being tired of the manuscript can easily make you think that it's done when it isn't.

On the other, a finished manuscript you've read dozens of times can seem boring because you've read it so many times.

If the *story* is boring you, that could indicate the story is, well, *boring*. Be objective and determine if this feeling is due to those countless re-reads, or if that scene has always felt blah. Be especially wary of scenes you tended to skip over during revisions because you felt they were "good enough" and didn't want to deal with them anymore. If you were skimming to get through it, you might want to reconsider that scene. Ask yourself:

What about the work feels wrong? If you can pinpoint specific problems, then you're not finished, even if the text is polished to perfection. The issue is likely a macro problem that has nothing to do with the quality of the prose, but a structural or story issue, such as, the pacing is slow in chapter nine, or the goal isn't clear in chapter six, maybe the front half is too long or the stakes are too low overall.

Has that scene or aspect ever bothered you before? Some scenes you know aren't right, but you ignore the warning signs. Often it's because you like the scene and want to keep it, even though you know deep down it should go. Listen to those nagging suspicions that you "ought to do something." Ignore that whisper that says, "No one will notice," or, "I can get away with it." That's a red flag you should fix it.

Uncertainty about a manuscript's readiness is normal, so don't fret if you have doubts. But also know you *can* cross the line between improving your manuscript and editing the life out of it. Stop before you change the text or story *just* so it sounds new.

Review it Like a Reader

Before you declare the novel finished, it's wise to let it sit for a few weeks and then read it straight through, same as if you'd bought it off the shelf. You're not a writer during this read; you're a reader, dying to find your next favorite author and a book you can't stop talking about.

In this session, the goal is to treat your novel the same as the toughest critics you'll ever have—your readers.

Go to wherever you most enjoy reading, using whatever device you prefer—hard copy or e-reader. Review your manuscript as if you were a reader who paid full hardcover price for this book (which means be tough—you deserve a great book for your money!).

When through, answer these questions as honestly as possible:

- ▶ Did the first line intrigue me?
- ▶ Did the first paragraph hook me?
- ▶ Did the first page make me want to read more?
- ▶ Did the first scene grab me?
- ▶ Was there a mystery or story question I wanted to see answered?
- ▶ Was there a suggestion or anticipation that something was about to go wrong?
- ▶ Did every scene make me want to read the next scene?
- ▶ Was there a reason to keep reading on every page?
- ▶ Did the chapters feel like they were going somewhere?
- ▶ Did the middle connect the opening goal and/or the core conflict goal?

- Did the stakes keep escalating and drawing me through the story?
- Were the mysteries and story questions interesting?
- Was I consistently learning new details about the story, world, plot, or characters?
- Was the voice consistent and enjoyable throughout?
- Were the characters consistent throughout?
- Was the final battle worth waiting for?
- Was the resolution satisfying?
- Would I tell my friends about this book (be honest)?

If you answered no to any of these, that's a red flag you still need a little more work in that particular area. Return to that session and re-do those exercises.

To check the general pacing and flow of the novel, answer the following questions:

- Did my mind ever start to wander?
- Did I notice any unnecessary scenes?
- Did I skim any scenes?
- Was I in a hurry to get through any scenes?
- Did I stumble over any of the text?

If you answered yes to any of these, that's a red flag the manuscript could still use some trimming or editing. Re-examine those scenes and determine what needs fixing.

If you *really* want to dig in for a final analysis, look objectively at the individual story pieces more than the novel as a whole.

Look at the Characters:

- Did I like the point-of-view character(s) and find them interesting and/or compelling?
- Did the characters and their actions seem real?

- Did the characters feel balanced in their views, attitudes, and opinions (or were they mouthpieces or yes men for the protagonist)?
- Did the characters behave in a credible fashion?

Look at the Plot:
- Did the plot make sense?
- Were the characters' goals clear?
- Did those goals advance the story?
- Were the goals believable?
- Were the stakes high or compelling enough to keep me interested and worried?
- Did the stakes seem genuine (not manufactured for the sake of drama)?
- Did the overall structure hold together?
- Was the plot predictable or did it surprise me (did it read as a fresh story or the same as other novels in its genre)?

Look at the Point of View:
- Did the narrative style fit the genre and book style?
- Did I feel connected to the point-of-view character(s)?
- Were there any points of view that felt unnecessary?

Look at the Description and Setting:
- Was I ever bored by too much backstory, exposition, or description?
- Did the world feel real and fleshed out?
- Was I ever uncertain about what something looked like?

Look at the Dialogue:
- Were the dialogue tags clear?
- Were the character voices different?
- Were there any talking heads in white rooms?

Look at the Pacing:
- ▶ Was the pacing good?
- ▶ Was I engaged in the story?
- ▶ Did I need a break at any time in the story?

If you find anything you'd like to tweak or fix, make those changes now. If everything checks out, declare your revision done!

It's Over!

Congratulations! You made it.

Even revising one aspect of a novel is a ton of work, but the results are usually worth it. Your characters should feel like real people and encourage readers to keep reading about them. If this was the only aspect of your novel that needed revision, good luck with the next step, whatever that may be for you.

But first, take some time to celebrate your victory. Revising a novel can be harder than writing it in the first place, and it's an accomplishment that should be rewarded. Go ahead, you earned it.

I hope you've enjoyed the workshops and that they helped turn your manuscript into a solid finished draft. If you've found this book helpful, please share with friends or leave reviews on your favorite sites.

Most of all, best of luck and good writing!

Janice Hardy
December 2017

Appendix

Quick-check analysis questions for easy manuscript review.

Common Red Flag Words

- Common self-aware red flag words: She knew, she realized, she felt, she thought. Not every instance will be a problem, but it's a good place to start the search.
- Common stimulus/response red flag words: when, as, before. Revise as needed so the stimulus comes first, then the character reaction.
- Common telling red flag words: Look for words such as: when, as, to (verb), which, because, to be verbs. These are often found in told prose.
- Common stage direction red flag words: Look for words such as, while, when, and as. These often connect multiple actions in one long (and confusing) chain.
- Common motivational red flag words: to (action), when, as, while, causing, making, because.
- Common emotional red flag words: In (emotion), and with (feeling).
- Common descriptive red flag words and phrases: Realize, could see, the sound of, the feel of, the smell of, tried to, trying, in order to, to make.
- Common passive red flag words: To be verbs—is, am, are, was, were, be, have, had, has, do, does, did, has been, have been, had been, will be, will have been, being.
- Common mental red flag words: realized, thought, wondered, hoped, considered, prayed, etc.

Analyze the Draft

- Weak goal-conflict-stakes structures: This could indicate a plot or narrative drive issue.
- Lack of character motivation: This could indicate a character arc or credibility issue.

- Sparse or missing descriptions: This could indicate a clarity or world-building issue.
- Heavy (or missing) backstory: This could indicate a pacing or character issue.
- Too many infodumps: This could indicate a pacing or show-don't-tell issue.
- Slow or uneven pacing: This could indicate a narrative drive or pacing issue.
- Lack of hooks: This could indicate a tension, narrative drive, or premise issue.
- Faulty logic: This could indicate a plausibility or plotting issue.
- Weak or missing foreshadowing or clues: This could indicate a tension, tone, or description issue.
- Areas that need more emotion: This could indicate an internalization issue.
- Weak characters and character arcs: This could indicate a character or internal conflict issue.
- Weak scene structure: This could indicate a plot or structure issue.
- Lack of narrative drive: This could indicate a pacing or goals issue.
- Inconsistent point of view: This could indicate a narrative, character, or show-don't-tell issue.
- Weak dialogue: This could indicate an infodump, dialogue, or character issue.
- Is the point-of-view character(s) likable or interesting enough to read about?
- Are their goals clear so there's narrative drive in the story?
- Do the characters seem real?
- Are there strong and interesting stakes?
- Is there too much back story, exposition, or description?
- Is the overall structure holding together?

- Does the opening scene have something to entice readers to keep reading?
- Do the scene and chapter endings entice readers to turn the page?
- Is the pacing strong?
- Are the plots, stakes, and goals believable?
- Does it read well overall?
- Do the sentences flow seamlessly or do any stick out and read awkwardly?
- Are the dialogue tags clear?
- Does the world seem fleshed out?

Analyze the Characters

- Do you have the right protagonist for this story?
- Do you have the right antagonist for this story?
- Do you have the right number of characters?
- Do you like the point-of-view character(s) or find them interesting?
- Do you care about these characters enough to read their story?
- Do the characters seem real?
- Are the characters believable in their roles?
- Are the characters flawed in ways that affect their decisions in the story?
- Do they have virtues that affect their decisions in the story?
- Do they have contradicting beliefs, both with themselves, and the other characters?
- How much physical description do you want?
- Are the main characters adequately described?
- Is there too much focus on physical details?
- Are the secondary characters described?
- How many details do you use to describe the various characters?
- Do the descriptions all fit the same format?

Analyze the Character Arcs
- What does the protagonist learn over the course of the novel?
- How does the internal conflict affect that growth? .
- What lie is she telling herself or does she believe at the start of the novel?
- When does she realize it is or isn't true?
- What does she want most of all as a person?
- Does the external plot facilitate her achieving this personal desire?
- What is she most afraid of?
- When does she face this fear?
- Where do the turning points of the growth occur? .

Analyze the Backstory
- Is the backstory relevant to the scene?
- Does this information help readers understand what's going on in this scene?
- Will knowing this information hurt the tension or mystery of the scene (or story)?
- What would be lost in this scene if you took the backstory out?
- Why do you want it in the scene?

Analyze the Theme
- What is the theme (or themes) of this story?
- Where examples of this theme are found in the novel?
- Where and how does the theme deepen the character arcs?
- How does the theme tie into the resolution of the novel?

Analyze the Point of View
- Is it clear who the narrator is?
- Is the narrator's voice consistent with the novel's tone?
- Is the narrator getting in the way of the story?

- Is the narrator revealing too much? Not enough?
- Are there any point-of-view shifts?
- Is the point of view consistent?
- Are there any scenes in a point-of-view style that differs from the rest of the manuscript?
- Is there too much filtering?
- Do characters know details they couldn't possibly know?
- Are any point-of-view characters oddly self-aware?
- Are there any inconsistent or out-of-the-blue emotional responses?
- Are any point-of-view characters stating the obvious?
- Are any point-of-view characters reacting before something happens?
- Are there any point-of-view scenes that are there only to show information the main characters can't witness?
- Do you use one point of view per scene (if it's not an omniscient point of view)?
- Is it clear when you've switched points of view?

Analyze the Internalization

- Is there too much internalization?
- Is there too little internalization?
- Does the internal thought clarify the dialogue or action?
- Does the internal thought show the point-of-view character's opinion on the situation?
- Does the internal thought provide necessary information without infodumping?
- Does the internal thought convey background information without telling?
- Are there internal thoughts in every line of dialogue?
- Are the internal thoughts often paragraphs long, and do they happen every time the point-of-view character thinks?
- Does the internal thought summarize a scene or idea at the end (or

describe it at the start before you show that scene or idea)?
- Are you repeating the same idea in multiple ways?

Analyze the Dialogue
- Do the characters sound like real people?
- Is the dialogue an actual conversation or two people stating information at one another for the reader's benefit?
- Are characters telling each other what they already know?
- Are there empty dialogue phrases?
- Is the dialogue advancing the plot or story?
- Are the dialogue tags clear?
- Are there too many dialogue tags?
- Are there any over-written or impossible dialogue tags?
- Are characters giving away too much information for no reason?
- Are you summarizing any conversations instead of dramatizing them?
- Is there subtext? Is it clear what's not being said?
- Is the language appropriate for the intended market?

Analyze the Voice
- Does each point-of-view character have his or her own voice and style of speaking?
- Can you tell who's speaking even without identifying the character by name?
- Can you get a sense of who the character is by the voice?
- Does the point-of-view character's outer voice sound like her internal one?
- Do characters use language suitable to their status, age, or cultural situation?
- Does the voice change depending on the situation?
- Do the non-point-of-view characters all sound the same?

- ▶ Are any of the character voices annoying?
- ▶ Are any of the character voices stereotyped or clichéd?
- ▶ Is there an overabundance of dialect?
- ▶ Does every character use the same vocabulary or is it varied? .
- ▶ Does every character speak with the same rhythm or pattern?

Glossary

Antagonist: The person or thing in the protagonist's path of success.

Backstory: The history and past of a character that affects his or her actions in a novel.

Conflict: Two sides in opposition, either externally or internally.

Core Conflict: The major problem or issue at the center of a novel.

Exposition: Narrative intended solely to convey information to the reader.

Filter Words: The specific words used to create narrative distance in the point-of-view character.

Genre: A category or novel type, such as mystery, fantasy, or romance.

Goal: What a character wants.

Hook: An element that grabs readers and makes them want to read on.

Inciting Event: The moment that triggers the core conflict of the novel and draws the protagonist into the plot.

Market: The demographic traits of the target audience for the novel, such as adult or young adult.

Narrative Distance: The distance between the reader and the point-of-view character.

Narrative Drive: The sense that the plot is moving forward.

Outline: The structured overview of how a novel will unfold, typically written as a guide before the novel is written.

Outliners: Writers who write with a predetermined outline or guide. They know how the book will end and how the plot will unfold before they start writing it.

Pacing: The speed of the novel, or how quickly the story moves.

Pantsers: Writers who write "by the seat of their pants," without outlines. They often don't know how the book will end or what will happen before they start writing it.

Plot: The series of scenes that illustrate a novel. What happens in the novel.

Point of View: The perspective used to tell the story.

Premise: The general description of the story.

Protagonist: The character driving the novel.

Query Letter: A one-page letter used to describe a novel when submitting a manuscript to an agent or editor.

Scene: An individual moment in a novel that dramatizes a goal or situation.

Series: Multiple books using the same characters and/or world.

Set Pieces: The key moments or events in a novel.

Setting: Where the novel takes place.

Sequel (1): A second book that continues where the first book leaves off.

Sequel (2): The period after a scene goal is resolved where the character reflects on events and makes a decision to act.

Stakes: What consequence will befall the protagonist if she fails to get her goal.

Stand-Alone Novel: A novel that contains one complete story in one book.

Structure: The framework a novel is written in, typically based on established turning points at specific moments in the novel.

Tension: The sense of something about to happen that keeps readers reading.

Theme: A recurring idea or concept explored in the novel.

Trilogy: A story that is told over the course of three books.

Trope: An idea or literary device commonly employed in a particular novel type.

Word Count: The number of words contained in a novel.

Thanks!

Thank you for reading Book One of my Revising Your Novel series, *Fixing Your Character & Point-of-View Problems*. I hope you found it useful!

- Reviews help other readers find books. I appreciate all reviews, whether positive or negative.
- If you enjoyed this book, you might also try the other books in my Revising Your Novel series: *Fixing Your Plot & Story Structure Problems*, and *Fixing Your Setting & Description Problems*.
- Also check out my in-depth Skill Builders series, *Understanding Conflict (And What It Really Means)*, and *Understanding Show, Don't Tell (And Really Getting It)*.
- For planning and developing a novel, try my Foundations of Fiction series, including *Plotting Your Novel: Ideas and Structure* and the *Plotting Your Novel Workbook*.
- I even write fantasy adventures for teens and tweens. My novels include The Healing Wars trilogy: *The Shifter, Blue Fire,* and *Darkfall* from Balzer+Bray/HarperCollins, available in paperback, e-book, and audio book formats.
- **Would you like more writing tips and advice?** Visit my writing site, Fiction University at Fiction-University.com, or follow me on Twitter at @Janice_Hardy.
- **Want to stay updated on future books, workshop, or events?** Subscribe to my newsletter. As a thank you, you'll receive my book, *25 Ways to Strengthen Your Writing Right Now*.

More from Janice Hardy

Award-winning author Janice Hardy (and founder of the popular writing site, Fiction University) takes you inside the writing process to show you how to craft compelling fiction: In her Foundations of Fiction series, she guides you through plotting, developing, and revising a novel. In her Skill Builders series, she uses in-depth analysis and easy-to-understand examples to examine the most common craft questions writers struggle with.

Understanding Show, Don't Tell (And Really Getting It) looks at one of the most frustrating aspects of writing—showing, and not telling. Learn what *show, don't tell* means, how to spot told prose in your writing, and when telling is the *right* thing to do. The book also explores aspects of writing that aren't technically telling, but are connected to told prose and can make prose feel told, such as infodumps, description, and backstory.

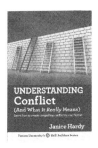

Understanding Conflict (And What It Really Means) looks at how to develop and create conflict in your fiction, and discusses the misconceptions about conflict that confuse and frustrate so many writers. The book also helps you understand what conflict really is, discusses the various aspects of conflict, and reveals why common advice on creating conflict doesn't always work.

Plotting Your Novel: Ideas and Structure shows you how to find and develop stories from that first spark of inspiration to the complete novel. It walks you through how to develop the right characters, find your setting, create your plot, as well as teach you how to identify where your novel fits in the market, and if your idea has what it takes to be a series. Ten self-guided workshops help you craft a solid plot. Each workshop builds upon the other to flesh out your idea as much or as little as you need to start writing, and contains guidance for plotters, pantsers, and everyone in between.

More from Janice Hardy

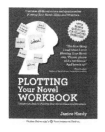

Plotting Your Novel Workbook is the companion guide to *Plotting Your Novel: Ideas and Structure* for those who like a hardcopy approach with easy-to-use worksheets. Its larger workbook format is perfect for writers who enjoy brainstorming on paper and developing their novels in an organized and guided format.

No more searching for ideas jotted down on bits of paper. No more losing notes just when you need them most. With more than 100 exercises for the novel-planning process, you can keep all your thoughts in one handy place.

Fixing Your Character & Point-of-View Problems takes you step-by-step through revising character and character-related issues, such as two-dimensional characters, inconsistent points of view, excessive backstory, stale dialogue, didactic internalization, and lack of voice. She'll show you how to analyze your draft, spot any problems or weak areas, and fix those problems. Five self-guided workshops show you how to craft compelling characters, solid points of view, and strong character voices readers will love.

Fixing Your Plot & Story Structure Problems guides you through plot and story structure-related issues, such as wandering plots; a lack of scene structure; no goals, conflicts, or stakes; low tension; no hooks; and slow pacing. She'll show you how to analyze your draft, spot any problems or weak areas, and fix those problems. Five self-guided workshops show you how to craft gripping plots and novels that are impossible to put down.

Fixing Your Setting & Description Problems focuses on setting and description-related issues, such as weak world building, heavy infodumping, told prose, awkward stage direction, inconsistent tone and mood, and overwritten descriptions. She'll show you how to analyze your draft, spot any problems or weak areas, and fix those problems. Five self-guided workshops show you how to craft immersive settings and worlds that draw readers into your story and keep them there.

Acknowledgements

As always, this book would not be here without the help and support of some amazing people.

I couldn't do this without my husband Tom. He's always there with the right words of encouragement—or the right amount of nagging—to keep me going when I need it.

Ann—a gal couldn't ask for a better crit partner. I'd be lost without your sharp eyes and insightful comments. You make me a better writer and I'm honored to call you friend.

And a big hug to all my beta readers on this book: TK Read, Chris Bailey, Lisa Bates, Trisha Slay, Beth Letters, and Dario Ciriello. You guys rock, and I appreciate all the help you gave me.

My Fiction University readers. You guys are the best, and your dedication to your craft, curiosity about the writing process, and your eagerness to learn are a constant source of inspiration for me. Hearing from you always makes my day.

Thank you all.

About the Author

Janice Hardy is the founder of Fiction University, a site dedicated to helping writers improve their craft. She writes both fiction and nonfiction.

Her nonfiction books include the Skill Builders series: *Understanding Show, Don't Tell (And Really Getting It)* and *Understanding Conflict (And What It Really Means)*, and the Foundations of Fiction series: *Plotting Your Novel: Ideas and Structure*, a self-guided workshop for planning or revising a novel; its companion guide, *Plotting Your Novel Workbook*; and the *Revising Your Novel: First Draft to Finished Draft* series.

She's also the author of the teen fantasy trilogy The Healing Wars, including *The Shifter*, *Blue Fire*, and *Darkfall*, from Balzer+Bray/Harper Collins. *The Shifter* was chosen by the Georgia Center for the Book for its 2014 list of "Ten Books All Young Georgians Should Read." It was also shortlisted for the Waterstones Children's Book Prize (2011) and The Truman Award (2011).

Janice lives in Central Florida with her husband, one yard zombie, two cats, and a very nervous freshwater eel.

Visit her author's site at janicehardy.com for more information, or visit fiction-university.com to learn more about writing.

Follow her at @Janice_Hardy for writing links.

Made in the USA
San Bernardino, CA
09 February 2018